THE UPSTART GUIDE TO
OWNING AND MANAGING A RESTAURANT

Roy S. Alonzo

UPSTART PUBLISHING
Specializing in Small Business Publishing
a division of Dearborn Publishing Group, Inc.

I sincerely thank my wife, Darlene,
to whom I dedicate this book,
for her cheerful encouragement.

This publication is designed to provide accurate and authoritative information in regard to the subject matter covered. It is sold with the understanding that the publisher is not engaged in rendering legal, accounting or other professional service. If legal advice or other expert assistance is required, the services of a competent professional person should be sought.

Executive Editor: Bobbye Middendorf
Managing Editor: Jack Kiburz
Associate Project Editor: Stephanie C. Schmidt
Cover Design: Paul Perlow Design

© 1996 by Roy S. Alonzo

Published by Upstart Publishing Company, Inc.,
a division of Dearborn Publishing Group, Inc.

Printed in the United States of America

10   9   8   7

Library of Congress Cataloging-in-Publication Data

Alonzo, Roy S.
    The Upstart guide to owning and managing a restaurant / Roy S. Alonzo.
        p.   cm.
    Includes index.
    ISBN 0-936894-89-X
    1. Restaurant management.   I. Title.
TX911.3.M27A427   1966
647.95'068—dc20   95-34406
                                                                          CIP

CONTENTS

Preface   *v*
Acknowledgments   *vi*

1   **The Restaurant Business**   *1*

2   **Start-Up Requirements**   *13*

3   **Strategy for Success**   *25*

4   **Planning To Be Profitable**   *46*

5   **Developing Menus That Sell**   *56*

6   **The Front of the House**   *72*

7   **The Back of the House**   *86*

8   **Operating Profitably**   *97*

9   **Managing Your Personnel**   *120*

10 **Maintaining Financial Control**   *133*

11 **Restaurant Marketing**   *146*

12 **Sanitation, Safety and Responsibility**   *172*

13 **If You Succeed—What Next?**   *183*

Appendix: Sample Business Plan and Loan Application
    for a Restaurant   *187*

Index   *215*

Preface

America's love affair with restaurants has never been greater, and it shows no signs of leveling off. Today, people dine in restaurants for many reasons—entertainment, to conduct business, to avoid cooking at home when they are tired or because they are working or traveling away from home. Over one-third of all meals consumed are eaten away from home. This presents great entrepreneurial opportunities for people who are attracted to the restaurant business.

According to National Restaurant Association data, the industry is comprised mostly of small businesses—there were almost 731,000 locations offering foodservice in the United States as of 1993. It is estimated that almost half of all adults are foodservice patrons on a typical day, and over 43 cents of the consumer's food dollar goes to meals and snacks away from home. The industry is a major employer—more than 9 million people are employed in foodservice, and employment is expected to reach over 12 million by the year 2005. In 1993, sales of restaurants of all types topped $236 billion.

Has the thought of becoming a restaurateur ever crossed your mind? If you enjoy dining out, entertaining guests or cooking, that would not have been an uncommon thought. Most people would like to earn their livelihood by doing something they enjoy.

The purpose of this book is to give readers a sense of what the restaurant business is like, to make them aware of what is required to enter it and to help them evaluate whether it is the right business for them. It is intended to acquaint readers with a logical course of action for starting a restaurant, should they decide to enter the business, and to give them insights and techniques for operating a restaurant successfully. The contents of this book are presented as a source of ideas, methods and procedures as well as a resource on where to find specific information.

The National Restaurant Association, institutions of higher education and restaurant and hotel chains have been very active in developing management systems and control procedures. However, even with a well-developed state of the art, many independent restaurants still function with inadequate controls, a shortcoming this book will address.

Laws vary from state to state and between the various levels of government. Where any laws are discussed in this book, it is only to make the reader aware of their existence. Consequently, nothing in this book is offered as legal advice or an interpretation of a law and should not be construed as such. Information of that kind should be obtained from attorneys and the appropriate government officials, just as advice on accounting and technical equipment matters should be sought from specialized professionals.

The mention of any product names in this book is done merely for illustrative purposes and should not be deemed an endorsement. Likewise, where products are mentioned, the omission of any products is not in any way a reflection on such products.

Finally, this book is intended to stimulate thinking about the restaurant business, answer a variety of questions and present an assortment of management tools that may be used to operate a restaurant. To those of you who may someday become restaurant owners, we wish you a full plate of success and an overflowing cup of happiness as you pursue your goals.

Acknowledgments

The contributions of many people and companies helped make this book possible. I would like to thank Market Forge Industries, Inc. of Everett, MA; Perlick Corporation of Milwaukee, WI; Starlite Diners, Inc. of Ormond Beach, FL; Jacob Licht, Inc. of Providence, RI; and Interstate Equipment Corp. of Manchester, NH for information, photos and drawings.

I would like to thank Ronald Cipullo, owner of Ronaldo's, in North Hampton, NH, and Kevin and Linda Van Etten, owners of the Country View Restaurant, in Greenland, NH, for sharing their business experiences.

For the use of photos, I would like to thank the New England Center of Durham, NH. I would also like to thank Bud Young, photographer.

THE RESTAURANT BUSINESS

The concept of a *restaurant*, as we know it, is a relatively recent one. It is asserted by some that the first restaurant in Europe was the Champ d'Oiseau, started by a chef named Boulanger in Paris in1765. Others claim the honor goes to another Parisian public eating house, La Tour d'Argent, opened in 1533. Whatever the case, it was not until after the French Revolution, in 1789, that the concept of a restaurant began to spread. Prominent chefs, who were once employed by the deposed wealthy, found themselves out of work and the more enterprising ones opened establishments to feed the public.

Prior to the 1700s, the only places where ordinary people could obtain a prepared meal were inns and taverns. The meals were not of the customer's choice and their price included a fee for lodging, which had to be paid whether or not the diner slept there.

The American Restaurant Scene

In colonial America, the establishment of taverns and road houses was decreed by law, as an aid to expanding the frontiers. The crude hostelries provided a simple meal and a sleeping accommodation, commonly shared with a fellow traveler.

As time progressed, a genteel class emerged in the colonies, and inns fashioned after those in England were built to serve them. The inns would accommodate guests who wished to dine only, but required them to pay for both food and lodging, as was the custom in England.

Few changes occurred in the public hospitality field after the colonies received their independence. It was not until the economy of the United States began to shift from agriculture to mining and manufacturing in the 1800s that significant innovations began to take place.

By the 1820s, eating establishments were being opened for the sole purpose of serving food and drink to the public. Such leaders as the Union Oyster House, founded in 1826 in Boston, Massachusetts, and Delmonico's, founded in New York City in 1827, were soon followed by others. The expansion of railroads created a great demand for eating establishments to accommodate transients. The demand was met with the gradual emergence of cafes, lunch rooms, tea rooms, cafeterias, coffee shops, diners and full-service restaurants.

Major changes occurred in the restaurant industry after World War II, as a result of the changing lifestyles of American people. The spectacular growth of the automobile industry and the building of the national highway system gave people greater mobility. Families that formerly could not afford one car, now had two or three. Americans took to the road in record numbers and restaurants popped up at every destination to serve their needs.

Some of the more important changes that impacted the restaurant industry in the second half of the twentieth century were the following:

- Franchising—fast food establishments made eating out convenient and more affordable.
- The growth of airlines made business and vacation travel commonplace.
- A large number of women entered the workforce, as a result of the need for a second income.
- The women's movement of the1970s and 80s helped to bring about more equitable compensation and gave women greater buying power.

- Eating out more often became routine for families with two working parents and for single working parents.

By the 1980s, there were restaurants for every pocketbook, palate and work schedule. People no longer ate out just because they were hungry—they were eating out for convenience, entertainment and a wide variety of business and social reasons. The restaurant industry had reached its age of majority.

What Attracts You to the Business?

Many people who like to cook or eat out are fascinated by the restaurant business, and some would like to own an eating establishment of their own. They enjoy meeting people and satisfying the palates of others with their culinary skills. Consequently, they view the business as a creative venture, with social and financial rewards.

It is true that there are many enjoyable aspects to the business—it can be creative, it does present the opportunity to meet interesting people and it allows many people to work at something they enjoy. Beyond that, restaurateurs are usually well-regarded by their customers and are commonly acquainted with the leaders of their community. These are attractive lures to the business, but they should not be the principal reasons for entering it.

Some Considerations

Not everyone who cooks well or likes to eat out should be in the restaurant business. As a matter of fact, you will probably have much less time available to eat out if you enter the business.

Restaurants can have excellent profit-making potential if they are run well; however, they are anything but your typical nine-to-five job. They require infinite attention to details, long hours, working on weekends and holidays, and occasionally dealing with nuisance customers. Does that make it bad? No, it depends on you—your lifestyle, your personal needs and goals.

It is not unusual today for professional and commercial people to experience the same demands from their work. Doctors, nurses, airline pilots, policemen, firemen, entertainers and increasingly people in the retail field—they all work odd hours and days, as well as weekends and holidays. When you own your own business, the redeeming feature for enduring such hardships is that you harvest the fruits of your labor—the profits are yours.

Can You Start a Restaurant with Limited Capital?

Is it possible for an entrepreneur with limited means to succeed in the restaurant business in this age of highly capitalized chain restaurants and stamped out franchises? Yes, if the owners operate within their means and take full advantage of the things that small businesses can do best—get to know their customers' wants and needs and serve them well. Following are profiles of two very different but highly successful small restaurants that typify the opportunities for small investors in the industry today.

Profile #1: A Breakfast and Lunch Restaurant

The Country View Restaurant, on Route 33 in Greenland, New Hampshire, is a prime example of how a modest start-up that focuses on the wants and needs of its clientele can succeed.

Faced with a layoff from his shipyard job, Kevin Van Etten was forced to make a career change. From time to time as he mulled his options, he half-heartedly flirted with the notion of starting a restaurant. He owned a piece of land on a busy state highway, and although he did not have any restaurant experience, he did have a long-standing fascination with the business. The more he thought about it, the more the idea appealed to him, so he decided to do it.

With the help of friends, he constructed the wood-frame building that was to become the Country View Restaurant. The simple design of the structure contributes a wholesome, rural ambience to the establishment. The restaurant's name derives from the beautiful view of a pasture with grazing horses, which can be seen from almost every seat in its dining room.

By opening day, the restaurant was outfitted with a combination of new and used equipment, decorated and seemingly ready to start—that is, until someone realized they had forgotten the menus which had to be hastily run off two hours before opening the doors to the public. It was also discovered that a coat rack was needed, so a hurried attempt was made to nail one to the wall—only to puncture a water pipe.

In the second week of operations, a moose wandered into the parking lot and created some excitement among the viewing diners. That incident gave birth to the restaurant's logo, a moose. Such were the trials of the start-up period—after that, however, the restaurant settled down and its steady pattern of growth began.

The Country View has 40 seats and 5 stools at the counter. It serves breakfast and lunch five days a week from 6:00 A.M. to 2:00 P.M. On Saturday and Sunday it serves only breakfast and closes at 1:00 P.M. Like everything that the restaurant does, its hours are tailored to the specific needs of its target market.

Now in its eighth year of operation, the restaurant still has three of its original employees and its staff has an average of five years of service. Their training and experience is evidenced by the fast pace of the waitpeople and the ability of the kitchen to keep up with the orders. The waitstaff makes every step count—no one goes into the kitchen empty-handed or comes out empty-handed. Although the operation is very efficient, its customers are never rushed and the waitstaff always has time for a personal word and an honest smile for them.

Kevin and Linda Van Etten are a husband and wife team. From the start, their skills complemented each other's. She had the restaurant experience that he lacked and he had the trade skills and business savvy. Today, she is the kitchen manager and he is the general manager. Their respective duties are well defined and, as a result, each functions smoothly.

The menu of the Country View ranges from lighter fare to hearty breakfast and lunch specialties, all of which are moderately priced. The owners have observed that many regular customers will watch their calories on week days, ordering lighter items such as bagels and coffee, but tend to splurge on weekends and order the specials, such as eggs Benedict or Belgian waffles with cream.

Asked what the secret of their success is, Kevin and Linda unequivocally respond, "Consistency—consistency of quality, of good portion sizes and of service. People like what they get here, and they want it to be the same every time." The customers of the Country View are very loyal. Once when the owners were on vacation, the furnace failed. Rather than allow the restaurant to close, some customers went out to the woodpile and brought in enough firewood to keep the old-fashioned woodstove that graces the dining room well-stoked all day.

The experience of this restaurant exemplifies how important it is to understand customers' wants and needs. The restaurant has waiting lines almost every day. Its clientele is a diverse aggregation of local residents, blue and white collar workers, weekenders on their way to the mountains or the seashore, and tourists who heard of the restaurant by word-of-mouth—the Country View does not advertise. Each group is unique, but the common denominator that attracts them all to the restaurant is the consistently good food and the pleasant service.

Profile #2: A Dinner Restaurant

Some people do not know what they want to do in life until they reach their thirties—other people never find out. Ron Cipullo knew he wanted to be in the restaurant business when he was a high school student working part-time in a restaurant. He liked it so much that after graduation, he stayed on as a cook. A few years later, he went to college to study restaurant management.

After receiving his degree he was determined to start his own restaurant, but had very little money. It seemed impossible until one day he discovered an old, run-down diner at Hampton Beach, New Hampshire, that was for sale at a distressed price. He scraped together all of his resources and bought it.

The peak season at the beach is short, so it is critical for businesses to be ready to open by Memorial Day. This created extreme pressure to get the facility ready to open in five weeks.

After throwing out a considerable amount of junk and giving the premises an intensive cleaning, painting and fixing, the restaurant was almost ready to open. Still missing, however, were booths that finally arrived on the day before the scheduled opening and had to be installed that night.

The restaurant opened on schedule—it was named Ronaldo's and featured creative Italian cuisine. Its hours of service were 4:00 to 10:00 P.M., seven nights a week.

On the first night of business 51 dinners were sold. Everyone involved with the restaurant's opening was elated because the only advertising that had been done was to hire an airplane to trail a banner, with Ronaldo's name and address on it, a few times over Hampton Beach.

The joy of the first night was short-lived, though, because only 19 dinners were sold on the second night, and 5 of those dinners were served to friends who came by just to give moral support. Ron says, "I was deflated and fraught with doubts that night—was the food or service not good? Were the prices too high? Did we misjudge the market potential?"

As time went by the volume grew, largely from word-of-mouth advertising, and gradually the doubts went away. By the end of the first summer, Ronaldo's had a waiting line almost every night of the week. This presented a bit of a problem, however, because the restaurant did not have a lobby or a bar, consequently waiting guests had to stand outside, rain or shine.

It was obvious that something had caught on. When asked what it was, Ron Cipullo answers, "The clientele that we cater to wants large portions of good tasting Italian food at reasonable prices, and they want creative dishes, not the stereotype Italian food with tomato sauce and hot spices." Seafood and white sauces are the mainstay of most entrees at Ronaldo's.

Surprisingly, business did not die after Labor Day, when most activities cease at northern beaches. It slowed down on weekdays, but on weekends they were filled to capacity. Ron discovered that he had established a steady local clientele, and that was the key to his survival in the business.

Eight years later, the restaurant is now located in a small shopping mall in the town of North Hampton. It is still convenient to vacationers at the beach and the local clientele, but it also benefits from the year round high traffic count on busy Route 1.

The 70-seat restaurant still has waiting lines and has served up to 400 dinners on a busy night. A few simple principles are the key to success at Ronaldo's—buy good food, prepare it properly, train employees well and maintain high standards.

Another factor that contributes to success at Ronaldo's is virtually every customer leaves with a substantial doggie bag. The doggie bags

Figure 1.1: Ronaldo's restaurant, which started with limited funds, built a "waiting-line clientele" by offering creative Italian cookery, in large portions, at reasonable prices. (Photo by Bud Young. Courtesy of Ronaldo's, North Hampton, New Hampshire.)

have become the hallmark of the restaurant. They generate a lot of conversation and increase customers' perception of value received at the restaurant.

Ronaldo's is a bootstrap operation that epitomizes the entrepreneurial opportunities in the restaurant business. It demonstrates that with determination, hard work and experience, a successful business can be started with limited finances.

Types of Restaurants

The restaurant industry offers a wide variety of opportunities for entrepreneurship—there is a type of restaurant for just about everyone who is attracted to the business. Early risers can operate breakfast and lunch establishments, and night people can run dinner restaurants. Below is a list depicting the wide variety of eating establishments in the restaurant industry. Each type of establishment has its own characteristics and clientele. (Note: This is just a partial listing;

obviously the types of restaurants possible are as varied as your imagination and your clientele's tastebuds.)

- Breakfast and Lunch
- Dinner restaurant
- BBQ restaurant
- Diner
- Truck stop
- Ice Cream restaurant
- Pizza restaurant
- Steak House
- Chicken restaurant

- Seafood restaurant
- Ethnic restaurant
- Coffee and Donut shop
- Buffet restaurant
- Tearoom
- Fast Food
- Sub shop
- Fish or Clam shack
- Vegetarian restaurant

The principal differences among eating establishments are the kind of food served, the style of presentation (table or counter service, or take-out), the atmosphere (formal or casual) and the price range.

A Typical Day in a Restaurant Manager's Life

The size of an establishment will determine the roles a manager may assume during the course of a day, as will the skills and interests of the manager. In a small start-up operation, a manager will do many things that in a large establishment would have to be delegated to other people.

A manager's duties in a small start-up restaurant could include: checking the previous day's receipts and preparing the bank deposit, inventorying the food supplies on hand, calling purveyors for competitive prices, placing orders, preparing work schedules, working on payroll, talking to salespeople, interviewing applicants for jobs, placing advertisements with media, repairing a broken piece of equipment, conducting meetings with employees, planning new menus, pricing menu items, calculating food and beverage costs, working up new sales promotional ideas, checking on quality and customer service, and working the dining room floor to greet the clientele.

Such a wide variety of duties can draw on the finest skills a person has to offer. Few other fields of employment offer such a diversity of

Figure 1.2: Diners are making a comeback. Reminiscent of the famous eateries of the forties and fifties, today's diners are brighter, more attractive and efficient. (Photos courtesy of Starlite Diners, Daytona Beach, Florida.)

activities. One thing is certain in the restaurant business—it is never boring.

Can Someone Else Manage Your Restaurant?

Yes, this has been amply demonstrated by the many successful restaurant chains one sees represented on the miracle mile in every community. Those organizations conduct in-depth training and have well tested policies that merely require execution by a competent manager.

In the case of smaller, independent restaurants, much depends on the knowledge and dedication of the hired manager. If that person is willing to make the same kind of personal sacrifices as the owner, it is very possible to have someone else manage your restaurant successfully. However, the degree to which such a person may succeed will depend a great deal upon the motivation and system of rewards you give them.

Is Restaurant Ownership for You?

The restaurant business is an entrepreneurial experience and as such has risks, disappointments, seemingly endless demands for time and money and no guarantee of success. External factors, such as bad weather, a natural disaster or a downturn in the economy, can impact your chances of success. Some people thrive on challenges that bring out their best qualities, but others feel insecure when faced with uncertainty.

The main question you must answer is, Are you cut out to be an entrepreneur? In other words, are you willing to risk your savings for a business? Would you be willing to take out a second mortgage on your house? Are you willing to borrow from friends and relatives? Is your family willing to undergo the lifestyle changes that might be required during the infant years of the business? Are you willing and able to work 12 hours a day, seven days a week, if necessary? Can you stand the uncertainty and pressure of the start-up period, which might be longer than expected?

Your passion for entering the restaurant business will be revealed in the answers to these questions. Most people prefer the stability of a nine-to-five job with a steady paycheck, and there is a great deal to be said for that. But, if you are the type of person who enjoys seeing your creation grow and thrives on challenges, in spite of unusual demands, the restaurant business may be an exhilarating and profitable experience for you. Only you can answer the question, Is it for you? The goal of this book is to help you operate successfully, should you decide to enter the business.

Action Guidelines

✔ Determine your tolerance for business risks by giving yourself an entrepreneurial test.

✔ Inventory your goals and priorities, then match them with a list of the benefits and rewards the restaurant business might provide, to determine if you will receive the satisfaction you seek.

✔ List your interests and skills and assess how closely they match up with those that are required or useful in the restaurant business.

✔ Research the industry in your locale and talk to restaurant people in noncompeting markets to get the benefit of their knowledge and advice.

✔ Read books and trade publications, and take courses pertinent to the restaurant business, to become acquainted with the field.

START-UP
REQUIREMENTS

Now that you've decided to become a restaurateur, the next step in the process is to determine what is required to open a restaurant. The requirements fall into four main categories:

1. Financial requirements
2. Personal requirements
3. Location requirements
4. Legal requirements

Financial Requirements

The amount of money needed to start a restaurant will vary depending on the size of establishment you have in mind, the geographic area in which it will be located and the condition of the local economy at the time. Obviously, leases and building costs are more expensive in prestigious areas than in others, and similarly, locations near attractions that draw large numbers of people, such as beaches and resorts, are typically more expensive. Construction costs are also more expensive in times of economic boom than they are in slack times.

The various expenses of starting a restaurant can be divided into three general categories for which you will need financing. They are:

1. *Initial Planning:* accounting and legal resources, market research and general and administrative expenses, such as telephone, duplicating, transportation and the services of consultants.

2. *Construction and Acquisition of Equipment and Supplies:* building or renovating a facility, purchasing and installing the necessary equipment, obtaining initial inventories and appropriate operating supplies.

3. *Pre-opening Expenses and Working Capital:* advertising, hiring and training a staff, cleaning up the premises after construction, and having adequate funds to meet payroll and pay other bills until your cash flow builds to where it can sustain current operating costs.

Sources of Financing

Traditional lending institutions are wary of granting a loan for a new restaurant if the applicant does not have a proven track record in the business. This is due to the historically high failure rate in the industry, by inexperienced people. Unless a borrower has adequate collateral to make a loan virtually risk-free, rigid lending practices will usually be applied by banks.

You will have to depend upon your own resources and those of partners or investors to a great extent. Following is a list of sources of funds, including some that are often overlooked:

- Soliciting partners
- Incorporating (selling stock)
- Personal savings
- Loans from relatives
- Collateralized bank loans
- Credit terms from equipment suppliers
- Credit terms from food suppliers
- Cash value of life insurance policies
- Loans from finance companies
- Small Business Administration loans
- Venture capitalist's loans

Personal Requirements

Beyond the personal requirements discussed in Chapter 1, there are skills that can enhance an entrepreneur's chances for success in the restaurant business. The skills required of an owner are largely determined by the extent to which he or she wishes to become involved in the daily operations of the business.

Some skills, such as cooking or bartending, are particularly useful when an employee does not show up on time or during an unexpected rush period. Likewise, some accounting knowledge is essential for understanding the books and for budgeting and filling in when the bookkeeper is on vacation. Public relations skills are vital when dealing with a disgruntled guest, and personnel management skills are necessary to motivate employees.

Must you have all of these skills yourself? Not necessarily. In large operations, many duties and responsibilities must be delegated to others because an owner or manager cannot be in all places at once. In smaller establishments where monetary constraints are a problem, it is common for the owner or manager to fill in wherever needed. The financial condition of a business will usually dictate how many hats an owner or manager will wear until the business gets established.

Some skills can be acquired by taking a job in the field to acquire experience or by taking courses at high schools or colleges. Other skills can be acquired from a paid consultant. Beyond that, free advice and training may sometimes be obtained from retired professionals who volunteer their expertise to fledgling businesses through the nonprofit Service Corps of Retired Executives (SCORE) organization. Their availability can be determined by calling your local Small Business Administration.

Location Requirements

A good location is critical to the success of a restaurant—extreme care must be taken when selecting a site. Many locations will not have the right demographic makeup or the right zoning for your business. Others may appear ideal but may have environmental problems or historical restrictions.

Accessibility to your target market is important. If customers will be arriving by car, the location must provide adequate space for convenient and safe parking. The restaurant should be located near tourist attractions if you wish to attract tourists. If you intend to cater to business people, it should be within a few minutes of their workplace. Choosing a good location is perhaps the most important task in the entire process of starting a restaurant. Site selection is discussed in detail in Chapter 3.

Legal Requirements

There is a public trust in the food service business that involves the health and safety of the consuming public. People dine in restaurants with the expectation that the food they eat will be wholesome, that it will be properly served and that they will not become ill from the experience. Consequently, the restaurant industry is tightly regulated by governmental agencies and without all of the necessary licenses, permits and approvals, you cannot open your doors for business.

There are three levels of control for restaurants—federal, state and local (city, town and county). The federal laws apply uniformly in all 50 states and the District of Columbia, but the state and local laws vary considerably from state to state and from one jurisdiction to another.

Early in the planning stage of your project, you should consult with the appropriate officials at all three levels of government to determine the specific requirements that apply to your situation. Moreover, you should remain in contact with those officials throughout your start-up process to assure you are progressing properly toward the satisfaction of all requirements. For the addresses of licensing commissions and other agencies, see *State Administrative Officials Classified by Function 1993–94,* in the reference section of your local library.

State and Local Requirements and Controls

On a day-to-day basis most of a restaurant's dealings are with local and state agencies. They typically involve adherence to the health code, liquor laws and public safety.

Food Service Licenses

All states have food service sanitation codes that require restaurants to obtain food service licenses before they can open for business. The name of this license may vary from state to state; some call it a health permit (Massachusetts calls it an Innholder/Common Victualler license), but no matter what the name is, the intent is the same—to ensure that food service establishments are operated in a sanitary and safe manner that complies with the food sanitation codes.

Without such a license, restaurants cannot sell food to the public. Furthermore, if at any time after opening, a restaurant fails to comply with the requirements of the food service sanitation code, its license may be revoked. Licenses are issued for one year at a time.

State and local public health authorities cooperate closely with each other on public health matters. In some jurisdictions, local health departments administer inspections of restaurants and issue food service licenses subject to approval by the state public health department. In others, state public health officials administer all aspects of the food sanitation code.

The typical process for obtaining a food service license is as follows:

1. Advise local officials of your proposed restaurant.
   - Building inspector
   - Planning board
   - Zoning board
2. Submit floor plans of your restaurant to the local health department, which will advise you if it is necessary to submit them to the state health department. Call to make an appointment to bring in the plans for review.
   - The placement of all major equipment must be shown, as well as the location of sinks and restrooms. A list of materials to be used for floors, walls, ceilings and food contact surfaces should be included.
   - A copy of your food and beverage menus must also be included.
3. Complete and submit a license application with the appropriate fee to the local or state health department, as directed.
4. Call the health department for a preopening inspection at least seven days prior to your planned opening date.
5. If all goes well with the preopening inspection, a food service license will be issued and periodic inspections will follow.

When planning a restaurant, particular attention should be paid to toilets and hand-washing facilities, sewage disposal, plumbing, lighting, ventilation, dish-washing and glass-washing facilities and all work surfaces. These are areas of vital concern to public health authorities.

Fire Permits

Fire safety is just as important as food safety—a restaurant cannot open for business until it has been issued a fire permit. The state fire marshal's office and local fire departments work hand in hand, but as a rule, it is the local fire departments that do the on-site inspections.

The local fire department places a limit on the number of patrons allowed into a restaurant. That capacity is determined by square footage and other factors contained in the state and local fire codes, which are modeled after the National Fire Protection Code.

Local fire departments issue permits upon passage of an inspection that includes, but is not limited to, the following items:

- *Clearances:* Gas-fired and other fuel-burning equipment must be installed with specified clearances from walls, ceilings and floors.

- *Exits:* There must be the correct number of exits, in the right locations, with no obstructions in the pathway and with illuminated exit signs above them. External exit doors must swing outward and be mounted with crash bars.

- *Fire Detection:* Smoke detectors and appropriate fire suppression systems (such as sprinklers, CO_2 and dry chemical) must be in place, as well as an emergency lighting system.

- *Sprinklers:* Must not be covered, blocked or otherwise impaired from performing as intended.

- *Fire Extinguishers:* An adequate quantity and type must be correctly placed throughout the premises. Usually, they must be located within 75 feet from any point, have a particular rating and be visible.

- *Electrical:* All electrical work must conform to applicable building codes and be done by licensed electricians, using approved materials. There must be an adequate electrical supply to safely meet the load required by the equipment and other electrically powered systems.

- *Flammable Liquids:* The storage, use and disposal of any flammable liquids (such as cooking oils) must be by approved means. Cooking equipment that utilizes combustible liquids must be protected by fire hoods with built in suppression systems.

- *Storage:* Aisles of at least 36 inches should be provided between shelves. Approved metal containers must be provided for debris or other combustible materials.

- *Miscellaneous:* Chimneys, heating equipment and vent systems must meet code requirements.

Building Permits

In most communities, it is necessary to check with several other agencies before applying for a building permit. Following is a typical sequence of events for obtaining a building permit and a Certificate of Occupancy:

1. Check with the Zoning Board to determine whether the zoning at your proposed location will allow a restaurant.

2. Obtain a site approval from the Planning Board. This is an important step if your restaurant is going to serve alcoholic beverages, because this is when public hearings will be held and abutters may voice objections to your plans. It is best to know of any objections early on. The board will consider such things as impact on traffic conditions and environment.

3. Next, a plan review meeting is held with an official from both the building and the fire department present. They will review the plans in detail, paying particular attention to the structural integrity of the building, the occupancy capacity for which it is rated, fire detection systems and conformance to all applicable codes.

4. Finally, formal application is made for a building permit.

If everything checks out well in the above stages, a building permit is issued and construction may be started. From this point on, the building inspector will make periodic inspections of the construction or renovation to determine compliance with codes. You must use licensed electricians and plumbers.

When the construction is completed, the building inspector and the health inspector will make a final inspection and upon passage of that inspection, a Certificate of Occupancy is issued to the owner of the business.

Other State and Local Departments

A restaurant must register its name and comply with state's labor laws, handicap access regulations and environmental regulations. It must also collect sales or meals taxes as may be required. For specific details on what is required, you should check with the appropriate agencies in your state.

- *Secretary of State:* To register the name of the business and to incorporate if that is the legal form of business chosen.
- *Commission on the Handicapped:* To inquire about accessibility requirements for new construction and renovations.
- *Bureau of Weights and Measures:* For inspection of any scales to be used in commercial trade.
- *Department of Revenue:* For information on sales taxes or meals taxes that may have to be collected.
- *Signage Commission:* Many communities now have an agency that controls signage and requires that a permit be obtained before a sign may be installed. They are primarily concerned with the size (square footage) of the sign, its height from ground level and the type of illumination planned for it.
- *Historical Commission:* Should you have plans to utilize a designated historical building for your restaurant, you may not be able to do the things you want with it.
- *Wetlands Commission:* Swamps and marshes are protected lands. If you are looking at a property for your restaurant site that contains wetland, you may not be able to drain it or fill it in for your parking lot. Inquire first.

In recent years, water supply and septic systems have come under much tighter control, as has the disposal of hazardous materials.

These are important matters to investigate when buying a property, particularly in suburban areas where wells and septic systems are common. Also beware of underground fuel tanks that may have to be removed at considerable expense.

Liquor Licenses

If you plan to sell alcoholic beverages in your restaurant, you will want to investigate the availability of a liquor license, early on. Many restaurant plans have been aborted because a liquor license was not available at the intended site.

All states require a liquor license to sell alcoholic beverages. Liquor laws vary from state to state, but they all have regulations governing what you can sell, where you can sell it, when and to whom you may sell it, and how you may advertise and promote it.

The availability of licenses also differs from state to state. In some they are more difficult to obtain than in others, due to the number of licenses already in existence in relation to the size of the population. In other states they are readily issued as long as the applicant and the premises meet the requirements for a license. Applicants for liquor licenses are checked thoroughly. Of greatest concern to state liquor control boards is an applicant's ability to obey laws and be financially responsible. The general requirements for a liquor license are that the applicant must:

- be 21 years of age or older.
- be financially responsible.
- have good moral character.
- be an American citizen.

The license for a restaurant that sells alcoholic beverages for consumption in the licensed premises only is called an *on-premise* license (as opposed to an *off-premise* licensed business, such as a liquor store). There are different types of on-premise licenses—beer only, beer and wine, and all alcoholic beverages. The effective term of a license is one year and it applies to only one specific location.

Allowing for variations from one jurisdiction to another, liquor laws typically cover the following items:

- Types of licenses available, fees and the application process
- Requirements for acquiring a license
- Hours and days of operation
- Proximity to churches, schools and hospitals
- Who may be employed in a licensed establishment
- Who may not be served alcoholic beverages
- Change of ownership or managers
- Changes or alterations to the licensed premises

All states have an alcoholic beverage control agency. In some states, only the state agency can issue a liquor license. In others, cities are allowed to issue a liquor license, provided the state agency approves the issuance of the license.

There are two categories of states as regards governmental control of the liquor business. They are referred to as *license states* and *control states*. In a license state, liquor products are distributed by private wholesalers, which have salespeople that call on restaurants and bars. In a control state, restaurants must buy their liquor products from state liquor stores or warehouses. There are 18 control states and each has its own regulations and ways of doing business.

Federal Requirements and Controls

The federal control agencies are the Department of Labor, the Internal Revenue Service and the Bureau of Alcohol, Tobacco and Firearms (BATF).

The Department of Labor administers the provisions of the Fair Labor Standards Act. Its principal concerns are compliance with the federal minimum wage laws and discriminatory practices. Where state and federal minimum wage levels are not the same, the higher of the two minimum wage rates prevails. Most of a restaurant's dealings on labor issues are conducted with state labor departments.

The Internal Revenue Service requires businesses to obtain an Employer Identification Number (EIN). This is done by filing IRS form number SS-4. It also requires restaurants to pay estimated federal income taxes on a quarterly basis. Employers are required by the IRS to withhold federal income taxes, Social Security (FICA) taxes and

Medicare taxes from their employees' pay. All such withholdings must be forwarded to the IRS by the 15th day of the following month, by either making an electronic deposit directly to the IRS or by making a deposit at your local commercial bank, using Federal Tax Deposit Form 8109. To calculate payroll withholdings, an employer should refer to IRS Circular E, Employer's Tax Guide.

Special Occupational Tax Stamp

If you plan to sell alcoholic beverages in your restaurant, you will need to obtain a Special Occupational Tax Stamp from the BATF, a division of the Treasury Department. Without that stamp, a restaurant cannot legally sell alcoholic beverages. The Special Tax Stamp is a receipt for payment of the Special Occupational Tax, not a federal license, and it does not confer any privileges on the retail dealer.

The law defines a retail dealer as "a person who sells alcoholic beverages to any other person other than a dealer." This includes all restaurants that sell alcoholic beverages for on-premise consumption. The Special Occupational Tax must be paid each year, on or before July 1.

For complete details on the federal liquor laws and regulations, call your nearest BATF office and ask for the free booklet, ATF P 5170.2 (8/89).

Action Guidelines

✔ Consult an accountant familiar with the restaurant business and an attorney familiar with the requirements for obtaining licenses and opening restaurants.

✔ Obtain specific information on the requirements for opening a restaurant in your location by doing the following:

1. Contact your local regulatory agencies:
    - Public Health Department
    - Liquor Commission (only if you plan to serve alcoholic beverages)
    - Building Department
    - Fire Department

2. Contact your state regulatory agencies:
    - State Public Health Department
    - Alcoholic Beverage Control Board (only if you plan to serve alcoholic beverages)
    - Secretary of State
    - State Department of Finance and Taxation

3. Contact the Bureau of Alcohol, Tobacco and Firearms

4. Contact the Internal Revenue Service

✔ Estimate the approximate costs of starting the type of restaurant you have in mind and match this with your possible sources of funds, using the resources described in this chapter.

STRATEGY FOR SUCCESS

A common misconception about restaurants is that they can endure the worst of economic times and even survive poor management, because people always have to eat. To the contrary, the facts show that many restaurants fail each year. But at the same time, some restaurants do extremely well and reward their owners handsomely. Why the difference?

Business scholars have studied the ingredients of success for a long time, but to date no one has come up with a formula that works in every case. The best you can hope for is that with training, experience, good planning and a lot of hard work you stand a chance of succeeding. It is possible, however, to increase your chances of success by learning from the experience of others.

Why Some Restaurants Fail

Of all new businesses, 80 percent fail within the first five years of their existence and restaurants are no exception. The two main causes of failure are undercapitalization and lack of knowledge about the restaurant business.

Simply put, *undercapitalization* means "not having enough money to do the job." It usually results from not having a financial plan when entering a business. Some entrepreneurs use all of their funds to construct their restaurant and do not have enough money left to meet their bills during the start-up period. Overspending on new equipment or renovations, rather than phasing in changes gradually as cash flow increases, is a common mistake. If a prospective restaurateur does not have enough capital to enter the business safely, it is best to hold off until the capital position is improved.

Lack of knowledge of the business covers a broad spectrum of things from not possessing any of the required skills to not knowing customers' wants and needs. It is essential that some training or experience be acquired before attempting to enter the field. Money alone cannot buy profitability. Some investors with adequate funds attempt to enter the restaurant business, but lack the interest or ability to manage it properly and unfortunately wind up with losses instead of profits.

Close supervision and sound policies are required because a restaurant business is made up of so many details which, if not properly tended to, can ruin it. Owners must constantly monitor their operations and look for weak spots that need improvement.

The following recommendations will help you stay in business:

1. Broaden your knowledge of the restaurant business as much as possible through:
   - personal research,
   - reading trade journals and books on the hospitality field,
   - obtaining information from food and beverage salespeople, and
   - attending professional seminars and taking useful courses.

2. Conduct a feasibility study before buying an existing restaurant or starting a new one.

3. Seek guidance from a reputable accountant and lawyer, preferably ones who are well acquainted with the restaurant field.

4. Join local professional associations and network with other, noncompeting restaurants owners.

5. Stay current—obtain information on new products, trends and promotional ideas from your suppliers and other educational resources.

6. Develop a financial plan (cash-flow budget) for your first year in business.

7. Compare your actual performance against your plan at frequent intervals during the year and make adjustments where necessary.

8. Control the following profit-centers carefully from the outset of the business:

   • *Purchasing*—Establish specifications for each product (purveyor, brand, size, maximum and minimum stock levels).

   • *Receiving*—Count and inspect all incoming shipments for proper quantity, quality and pricing before signing invoices.

   • *Storing*—Put away all incoming shipments of foods, beverages and supplies, in secured storage locations. A minimum of keys to locked storerooms should be issued, and only to key personnel.

   • *Issuing*—All shipments received and all issues of products from inventory should be recorded in an inventory book.

   • *Inventory*—A physical inventory (actually counted) should be taken at least once a month, to verify the accuracy of the balances on hand shown in the inventory book.

   • *Standard Recipes*—Use standard recipes to insure consistency of product quality.

   • *Portion Control*—Establish standard portion sizes and utilize measuring tools, such as scales and numbered scoops and ladles to insure consistency of production cost and customer satisfaction.

   • *Cashiering*—Make sure every product served is accounted for, according to your policies. If you want to give away a complimentary meal, fine, it is your business. But no one else should have the right to give away your profits.

9. Know your customers. The better you know them individually and as a class the better you will be able to serve them. Here are some ways of viewing your customers:

Age	Type of jobs
Sex	Education levels
Income	Type of transportation
Interests	Food and beverage preferences

10. Observe your customers' spending habits.

    • Where are they spending their money?

    • What are they buying?

    • How much do they tend to spend?

    • What time do they arrive? How long do they stay?

    • Do they come alone or with friends?

11. Make your customers feel welcome. Talk to them and get feedback.

12. Establish and adhere to responsible business practices. This will affect your relations with your community.

13. Keep up-to-date on laws and regulations that pertain to the restaurant business.

14. Advertise effectively to attract the type of clientele you desire.

15. Give your customers reasons to come back again soon. Develop a steady flow of menu specials and promotional events, and announce them on table tents and wall posters.

16. Price your menu competitively according to your particular style of service and serve high-quality food consistent with your prices.

17. Keep your premises clean and up-to-date.

Management should conduct periodic surveys of the restaurant to identify problems and anticipate possible causes of failure. Corrective actions should be taken as soon as possible, and they should be assessed shortly after their implementation to determine the effectiveness of an action.

For example, suppose Restaurant A is losing customers to Restaurant B, a new competitor who features a piano player in their dining room. So in response, A begins to offer musical entertainment. After two weeks A reviews the situation and finds that sales are still declining and on top of that, their profits have shrunk because they are now paying for the entertainment. The corrective action must be assessed. Possibly, they have engaged the wrong type of entertainment for their particular clientele. Or, it may be that the competitor's entertainment is not what is drawing the customers away. It might be that the quality of A's food has slipped, or any number of other reasons. The point that A must recognize is the corrective action has not achieved the desired result and therefore must be modified.

You should be your severest critic, because no one else cares as much as you do about the success of your restaurant. If it is going to stand a chance of succeeding, its management must be honest and objective in its appraisal of how good the restaurant is performing.

Start from Scratch or Buy?

There are two ways to enter the business: one is to start a new restaurant from scratch; the other is to buy an existing one. Neither way is a surefire guarantee of success. However, having a knowledge of the factors involved in each approach can significantly improve your chances of succeeding.

Should You Start a New Restaurant?

People who have a truly unique concept and the necessary money to finance their idea will probably want to start a new restaurant. Especially since extensively renovating a going restaurant would eradicate most of the savings associated with buying an existing business, and oftentimes compromises the initial plan.

With a new restaurant, you will have to do everything that would have already been done in an established restaurant—but you will be able to do it your way.

You will have to address all of the responsibilities associated with a business start-up. For example, you will have to establish an organization, find a suitable location, develop your menus, determine prices, project sales, purchase equipment, develop a floor plan, select your decor, develop a service system, plan your entertainment and hire and train a new staff. If you have a brand new concept, you will also have to advertise it aggressively until you achieve name recognition.

When all of these things are done, you will open your doors to the public and hope your new restaurant will be a success, but you can never be sure until the operation is tested in the marketplace against the competition.

The typical progression of start-up activities for a restaurant project with adequate funding in place is depicted in Figure 3.1. In cases where external financing is required, the project would be planned up to the point of estimating its cost and potential return before approaching investors or lenders. The cost of the project must be reasonable in terms of its potential return, otherwise it will not attract investors. If the estimated cost is too high, you will have to loop back in the process and make the necessary changes.

The talents, financial resources and experience of the principals make every start-up situation unique; however the basic process tends to be the same. It is advisable to engage the services of an accountant, a lawyer and a foodservice consultant at the outset of the project.

The actual steps required in a project will be determined by its size and scope. If new construction for a large restaurant were required, you would want to bring in an architect at the beginning of the process. On the other hand, if you were planning a small luncheonette to go into a rented space, you would not need an architect at all. With the proper approvals and help from some equipment salespeople, you could plan your own layout and, given the necessary skills, do most of the general work yourself. Electrical, gas and plumbing work should be subcontracted to licensed tradesmen, and frequent consultation with building, fire and health inspectors is prudent.

Should You Buy an Existing Restaurant?

The biggest advantages to buying an existing restaurant are that it comes with (a) an immediate cash flow, (b) an experienced staff and (c) production and service systems that are in place. In effect, you save the start-up costs of a new business—but care must be taken to assure you do not inherit unwanted problems, such as an irreparable bad reputation, an incompetent staff, outdated equipment or a short lease. Be aware also that if the success of an existing restaurant is intricately tied to the image of the present owner or chef, there is no guarantee its success will continue after the business changes hands.

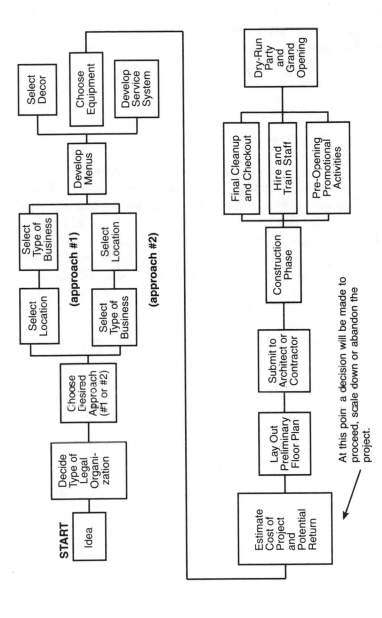

Figure 3.1: A typical flow chart of activities for a start-up restaurant business. Legal, accounting and food service consultants should be engaged early in the process.

Arrange to have an equipment specialist accompany you when you inspect a restaurant that you are seriously considering buying. The small cost for this service is well worth it. Check the age and condition of the equipment to determine if a great deal of it is obsolete or about to fail and consider how appropriate the equipment will be for producing the menu you have in mind.

How Much Should You Pay for an Existing Restaurant?

There is no one rule of thumb. The answer to this question will vary with the facts of each situation. For instance, if you were considering buying a restaurant in its entirety—that is, a going operation with a successful track record and an attractive cash flow—it would be valued one way; whereas, if you intended to buy just the assets of a business, they would be valued quite differently. In the first case, the price would be based on the value of the assets plus the value of a proven income stream. In the second case, the price would be based solely on the value of the assets, which, unless utilized properly, may or may not ever produce profits.

Likewise, a restaurant in an extraordinarily good location will command a substantial premium over the price of one in a mediocre location.

Potential buyers may use several techniques to assess an existing restaurant and use the results to determine a high and low end of an acceptable price range, within which you can dicker. This is an area where you should work closely with your accountant. Four of the more common methods are listed below:

1. *Comparable Values of Similar Going Concerns*—This method arrives at a value based on what similar restaurants have sold for.

2. *Reproduction or Replacement Value*—This method is based on the open-market cost of reproducing the assets of the business. It is most useful when only the assets are being purchased.

3. *Earnings Approach*—Here the focus is on the annual earnings of the business. Earnings can be used to calculate your potential return-on-investment; however, some cautions are important.

Earnings can vary with methods of accounting. For example, in the case of a sole proprietorship, where an owner may work but is not an employee and is not paid a salary, the business's earnings would appear much higher than they should be. Also, if economic conditions have shifted and are now declining, past performance may not be a good indicator of what can be expected in the future.

Some people will use a multiple of five or six times annual earnings to establish a theoretical value that fits their amortization timetable, while others with a limited life concept will seek a faster pay off. However, in the end you should regard earnings as just one measure that must be looked at alongside the others.

4. *Book Value*—Essentially this is the "adjusted book value" of a restaurant, arrived at by subtracting total liabilities from total assets and adjusting for any intangibles such as goodwill. Although the data is based on a firm's most recent balance sheet, the value of the assets should be tested for fair market value and, if necessary, so restated.

How Much Should You Pay for Rent?

The concept of time and place are all important. *Time* refers to what is happening at a location within a given period. For instance, a storefront one block away from the site of a major event like a World's Fair or an Olympic stadium during a given year will fetch a far greater rent than it would at another time. *Place* refers to location. A site between two high volume anchor stores in a prestigious mall would garner a higher rent than a store in a less desirable area.

Rent is also influenced by factors other than the traffic count. The age of a building and the desirability of its address, as well as the provision of amenities, such as heat, light, water, parking and snow removal, will affect rents. When expenses such as property taxes, insurance and maintenance are paid by the lessee, the lease is referred to as a triple net lease. A National Restaurant Association publication, *Restaurant Industry Operations Report, 1993,* shows occupancy costs (which include rent, property taxes and insurance) for full-menu, table service restaurants that sell both food and beverages averaged 4.5 percent to 9.5 percent of total sales that year.

When budgeting for expenses, it is important to be conservative in estimating total sales so as to not overstate the amount allocated for expenses that are forecast as a percentage of sales.

Evaluate Before You Invest

It is critical that you research an existing restaurant thoroughly before buying it. Figure 3.2 is a checklist for surveying an establishment. It will draw your attention to areas that might easily be overlooked.

Figure 3.2:

Checklist for Surveying an Existing Restaurant

Areas to Evaluate   **Comments**

1. Purchasing and receiving procedures

2. Storing and issuing methods

3. Equipment and layout
   a. Location of equipment
   b. Maintenance of equipment
   c. Suitability of equipment to menu

4. Functional aspects of equipment
   a. Ability to clean
   b. Attractive design
   c. Easy to operate

5. Food preparation methods
   a. Quality control—recipes
   b. Use of premixes
   c. Portion control
   d. Presentation

6. Inventory
   a. Item popularity
   b. Product availability
   c. Price range
   d. Turnover rate

Figure 3.2, Checklist, *continued.*

Areas to Evaluate	**Comments**

7. Personnel
   a. Staffing
   b. Duties and responsibilities
   c. Grooming
   d. Uniforms
   e. Productivity
   f. Morale

8. Labor
   a. Turnover of employees
   b. Training on the job
   c. Overtime policies

9. Food and beverage costs
   a. Standard recipes
   b. Inventory control records
   c. Pilferage control
   d. Cost percentages

10. Food presentation methods
    a. Size of portions
    b. Garnishes
    c. Variety of colors, textures

11. Service system
    a. Order taking
    b. Pickup system
    c. Guest check controls
    d. Delivery system

12. Dining room and lounge
    a. Number of servers
    b. Tables per station
    c. Style of service
    d. Decor
    e. Type of clientele
    f. Average guest check size

Figure 3.2, Checklist, *continued.*

<u>Areas to Evaluate</u> **<u>Comments</u>**

13. China, glassware, utensils, paper supplies
    a. Backup inventory supply
    b. Inventory-taking procedures
    c. Reorder policies

14. Advertising and sales promotion
    a. Types of ads, frequency
    b. Media used
    c. Effectiveness of ads

15. Sanitation
    a. Inspection policies
    b. Training
    c. Equipment
    d. Method of supervision

16. Safety
    a. Fire extinguishing equipment
    b. Fire exits
    c. Fire retardant materials
    d. Emergency lighting
    e. Fire detection systems

17. Communications
    a. Lines of authority
    b. Supervision
    c. Policy manual

18. Accounting Controls
    a. Food cost controls
    b. Beverage cost controls
    c. Labor cost controls
    d. Controllable general expenses

19. Physical appearance of property
    a. Building, exterior and interior
    b. Furniture, fixtures and equipment
    c. Obsolescence factor

Obtain Professional Assistance

Engage experts to help you evaluate a restaurant—talk to bankers, suppliers and repairmen. They can give you information about less obvious parts of the business. Also talk to patrons, neighbors and anyone else that may have information about the business. Try to find out how the restaurant has been doing in regard to sales, public image and customer satisfaction. But most of all, be sure to get your accountant and lawyer involved at this stage of your evaluation.

Insist that your accountant be permitted to examine the official books of the business. Check for outstanding bills if you buy the restaurant in its entirety. If deposits for future functions (banquets booked in advance) have been accepted by the current owner, adjustments should be made during the closing process. In addition, determine whether all tax obligations have been fulfilled and all taxes have been paid, or whether there are tax issues to be resolved with the IRS.

Closing the Deal

It is wise to hire an attorney who is familiar with the restaurant industry. If you do not know such a lawyer, contact your local bar association. Their referral service will give you several names to choose from. Have your attorney review all documents before you sign them. You will be encountering contractual matters that are beyond the ability of the average layperson to cope with. Be sure to make any agreements you enter into contingent upon your acquiring the necessary licenses and permits, because without the required licenses and permits you will not be able to open for business. To assure that everything is done properly and in your best interest, have your lawyer present at all signings.

Choosing a Legal Form of Business Entity

In general, the three most common legal forms from which you may choose are: the sole proprietorship, the partnership, and the corporation. Each has its advantages and disadvantages. Which legal form of business entity is best for you is a matter that should be worked out with your lawyer and your accountant. At issue will be how much money you have to invest, how much personal involvement in the business you wish to undertake, tax implications and liability and disclosure requirements.

Sole Proprietorship

The idea of not having a boss or committee meetings is very appealing to many people. The sole proprietorship is very popular because it gives the owner complete domination over a business. The owner can make the rules and set the policies, take time off at will or work long hours. Best of all, the owner doesn't have to split the profits with partners or stockholders, and the profits are taxed as if they were personal income. In addition, the owner enjoys prestige, hires and fires people and has final authority for everything.

Counterbalancing the above, the owner must carry the entire financial burden of the business and be competent at all of the roles he or she must assume. Beyond that the owner must deal with all of the business's problems alone. The greatest disadvantage of a sole proprietorship, however, is that it has unlimited liability. Everything of value that the proprietor owns is at risk if the business fails. In other words, if you end up owing money, creditors can come after your house, your car and all your other personal property.

Partnership

Partnerships function best when the partners have complimentary talents and each brings financial resources to the business. Small partnerships may enjoy some of the advantages of a sole proprietorship, except that everything you own, do or earn is shared with one or more partners.

The two most common types of partnerships among small businesses are the *general partnership* and the *limited partnership*. In a general partnership, all partners bear the burden of unlimited liability. In a limited partnership, there must be at least one general partner who runs the business and has unlimited liability, but an unrestricted number of others may be limited partners who have limited liability and are not required to take an active role in the operations of the business.

It is important to have a partnership agreement drawn up by an attorney and signed by all partners. The agreement should include, at the very least, the names of all partners, the amount of each partner's investment, the share of the firm's profits to which each partner will be entitled, the role and responsibilities of each partner in the operations of the business and what will happen in the event a partner dies or wants to sell his or her ownership share.

One partner's actions may jeopardize a business and create a liability that must be shared by all partners; therefore it is essential to know and trust implicitly the individuals with whom you become a partner. As a general rule, you have no reason to consider the partnership form of business, unless you need the skills or the funds of other people to launch your business.

Corporation

A corporation is defined as "a fictitious person" by the U.S. Supreme Court. Therefore, because you are a real person, you cannot be a corporation. A corporation is held to be a separate entity from yourself. You may, however, be a stockholder, a director, an officer or an employee of a corporation. Three or more persons are usually required to obtain a corporate charter, elect a Board of Directors, who direct the corporation, and appoint officers to run it. Following is a list of advantages of incorporating.

1. Raising additional capital for growth or expansion is easier than with a proprietorship or partnership.

2. Your personal assets are protected from seizure or attachment by corporate creditors.

3. Your liability is limited to your investment in the corporation (unless you misuse corporate funds or facilities).

4. Stock can be used as collateral for loans, whereas proprietorships and partnerships may have to use their personal assets.

5. Filing a Subchapter S election allows gains and losses to flow directly through to stockholders, so that they can be treated as personal income. (In this respect the Subchapter S corporation is like a partnership.)

Acquiring Additional Capital

A corporation may issue additional shares of stock without affecting the workings of the company because its owners are legally separated from the operations of the company. This is where the corporate form of business has a distinct advantage over other forms. A corporation can also obtain debt capital from professional lending institutions.

If a sole proprietor is an established member of the business community, is well networked in local financial circles and has an upstanding reputation, borrowing as a private individual may not present a problem. However, if you are new to a community, you will find it very difficult to borrow money for a restaurant. A sole proprietor cannot sell stock and must, therefore, borrow additional capital on the strength of his or her personal and business reputation.

A partnership may bring new partners with investment capital into the firm. However, finding the right persons to associate with is not always an easy matter. Extreme caution must be exercised because of the unlimited liability feature of a general partnership.

Selecting a Location and a Property

The words "location, location, location," are sometimes referred to as the three keys to success. Without a good location most fledgling businesses are doomed from their start, because the effort and funds required to offset the shortcomings of a poor site drain resources from more important aspects of the business.

The site analysis checklist (Figure 3.3) can be useful when evaluating restaurant sites. It can be very helpful to use a tape recorder for storing detailed information as you investigate potential sites. Not all items in the checklist are applicable in every situation.

Data may be obtained from tax offices, registry of deeds books, town or city clerks, Realtors and brokers, highway departments, chambers of commerce, as well as on-site inspections.

Figure 3.3:

Restaurant Site Analysis

Address of Site_____   Present Owner or Agent_____
City/State/Zip_____   Address_____
Lot No._____   City/State/Zip_____
Map Ref._____   Tel. _____
Date of Inspection_____   Asking Price_____

Physical Features of the Land:

Size: Approach—Visibility:
Shape: Accessibility to Target Market:
Slope: Clearance:
Expansion Possibilities: Zoning:
Utilities: Nearby Hazard or Blights:
   Water, Gas, Electricity   Parking Possibilities:
   Sewers   Snow Removal or Storage
Soil Conditions: Perc. Tests,   Space:
   Drainage

Economic and Community Features:

Economic Trend: Wage Trends:
Public Transportation: Competition:
Local Attraction: Income Levels:
Civic Promotional: Seasonal Features:
Agencies: Major Highways Nearby:
Labor Supply: Population—Number and
Traffic—Passing Daily: Makeup:
Auto Count: Fire and Police Protection:
Pedestrian Count: Food and Beverage Suppliers:

(continued)

Figure 3.3, Site Analysis, *continued.*

Physical Features of the Structure:

This is a partial list. Your REALTOR® *can supply you with additional information.*

Perimeter Dimensions:
No. of Rooms: Sizes
Traffic Flow Lines:
No. of Restrooms:
Flooring Materials:
Storage Possibilities:
Insulation:
Type of Siding and Roofing:
Electrical Service: Amps,
   Phase

Gas Service: LP or Natural,
   Size
Sewer: Municipal or Septic
   Tank
Water: Municipal or Well,
   Volume
Handicap Accessibility:
Heating/Ventilation/Air
   Conditioning:

Laws and Restrictions:

Zoning of Property:
Land-Use Laws: Environ-
   mental
Permits and Licenses
   Needed:
Building Restrictions:

Wetland Restrictions:
Building Height and Setback
   Requirement:
Lighting and Signage
   Requirement:
Parking Regulations:

Taxes

Property Tax:
Income or Business Tax:
Assessment Percentage:
City Sales Tax:

Meals and Lodging Tax:
State Sales Tax:
Water and Sewer Tax:

Cost of Property:

Land:
Building:

Necessary Improvements:
Total Investment:

Naming Your Restaurant

As with all businesses, names must be approved by and registered with the secretary of state of the state in which the business is domiciled. It is wise to submit three desired names in their order of preference because your first choice may already be taken. The names will be screened through a computer, and if no one else has already registered the name you want, you will get it.

The actual process of registering a business name is an easy matter. Simply obtain the appropriate forms from the secretary of state's office (in your state capital), fill them out specifying your desired names and return them to the secretary of state with a check for the stipulated fee. That is the legal side of selecting a name.

The other aspect of selecting a name, the public relations aspect, is equally as important. Thoughtful consideration should be given to your name because it can serve many purposes, the most prominent of which is to convey specific information to the public. Some examples are:

- La Casa Napoli—indicates it is an Italian restaurant.
- Fisherman's Landing—suggests seafood and a nautical decor.
- The State Street Grill—tells you where it is.
- The 24-Hour Diner—declares it is open all night.

Consider the most important message you want your name to convey in terms of who your target market is and what they want, then match their expectations.

Risk Management

A successful risk management program must include three things—acquiring adequate insurance, training your staff and setting sound company policies. It is advisable to have an insurance agent or broker design a complete insurance program for your business and discuss with you techniques for cost containment. Types of insurance available include:

Type of Insurance	Hazard Covered
Named Peril	Property coverage, limited to specifically named types of losses.
General Comprehensive Liability	Covers claims for bodily injury and property damage due to an accident.
Personal Injury Liability	Covers law suits due to false arrest, libel, slander, defamation of character and personal injuries.
Automobile Liability	Covers damages or injuries that employees incur while driving their car or a company car in the performance of company business.
Liquor Liability	Protects against suits resulting from damages or injuries to others by a person that became intoxicated in your establishment.
Property Damage	Covers buildings, inventory, equipment and fixtures against loss due to fire, smoke, explosion or vandalism.
Product Liability	Covers against suits based on damages or injuries resulting from a product that you served.
Fire	Covers damages to other buildings from a fire that originated on your property.
Workers' Compensation	Covers employees' medical and rehabilitation costs for work-related injuries.
Business Interruption	Reimburses you for expenses incurred and for revenues and profits lost as a result of unintended interruption of your business due to fire, major theft or illness of a key employee.
Bonds	Covers against law suits for financial loss incurred by others due to an act or default of an employee or to some contingency over which the principal may have no control.

Some carriers specialize in insuring food and beverage establishments. Their rates will vary according to the type of business, condition of the premises, degree of exposure to risks and your risk management program.

Action Guidelines

✔ List the relative merits of buying an existing restaurant, as opposed to starting one.

✔ Acquaint yourself with accountants and lawyers that have experience in the restaurant industry.

✔ Select the legal form of business entity that is most appropriate for your restaurant.

✔ Choose three names for your restaurant and check the availability of those names with the secretary of state's office in your state.

✔ Evaluate several potential sites using the restaurant site analysis chart contained in this chapter.

✔ Work with an insurance broker to develop a risk management program to meet the needs of your restaurant.

PLANNING TO BE PROFITABLE

Why Do You Need a Business Plan?

Careful planning is a key ingredient for the success of a new business—without it, a restaurant can only expect to react to crises, rather than avoid them or manage them effectively.

Although the most common use of a business plan is to persuade potential investors or lenders to finance your project, its primary value should be to assure you, the entrepreneur, that the enterprise is both feasible and potentially rewarding.

In the process of developing a business plan, you are forced to confront all of the issues that can spell success or failure. You are compelled to focus on what you wish to accomplish and how you intend to do it. Should there be any weaknesses in your plans, they will become evident.

The business plan can also serve as an action plan that can guide you through your start-up period and be a reference point against which you can compare your actual performance.

Finally, a well-written business plan will convey to its readers the assurance that you can think clearly and have the ability to run a restaurant successfully.

Accuracy Is Important

It is essential that your business plan be believable—be prepared to defend the statements you make. It is perfectly acceptable to present information in its best light, but inaccurate or incomplete information will be construed as undependable or deceptive by investors and lenders and will very likely deter them from participating in your project.

The most important reason for being accurate and complete is that you will need the most reliable information available to make sound decisions. Inaccurate information will mislead you and might cause you to make decisions that could lead to failure of the business.

Estimating Your Start-Up Costs

As with any business investment, the cost of the project is a primary concern in everyone's mind since the best of ideas are of little value if they cannot be funded. Knowing the cost, early on, can save a lot of wasted time and effort.

Information on costs can be obtained from a number of sources. On small jobs certain information can be obtained for free from vendors, but on larger projects that involve time and research, you should expect to pay a consulting fee for services rendered.

Equipment suppliers can provide you with working figures on dining room, kitchen and bar equipment. Commercial Realtors can supply cost data and advice on suitable rental properties for your venture. Architects and contractors, interested in getting your business, can give you ballpark figures as you consider the feasibility of your project.

Distributors of food, liquor, beer and wine products can assist you in estimating inventory costs. Since you may be one of their customers in the future, it is in their best interest to help you with your early planning. Wherever it is possible, cross check information with more than one source.

If your business is a sole proprietorship or partnership, you may have limited capital to work with; consequently, the matter of estimating start-up costs will happen in stages, starting with ballpark figures. As your ideas become better defined, your estimates will become more dependable. At each stage of the process, you must answer the question, Can I afford it? If you believe you can, you will proceed to obtain final figures and that might entail hiring a consultant to develop a reliable estimate for you.

If you do not feel you can afford the project, as the ballpark figures show it, you must go back to square one and scale down your ideas to a level that you can afford or abandon the project.

In the case of a corporation, the opportunity exists to raise additional funds through the sale of more stock. However, potential investors will scrutinize your business plan carefully and will want to be convinced of (1) the business's chances of success and (2) the anticipated rate of return on investment that they can expect.

The Business Plan

Business plans may vary in format, but certain kinds of information are expected to appear in all business plans. An outline of a typical business plan for a restaurant is shown in Figure 4.1 and is followed by explanations of the type of information that might appear in each section. (A sample business plan for a restaurant appears in the appendix.)

Figure 4.1:

Outline of a Business Plan

Cover Page
Table of Contents
Statement of Purpose

Part One: The Business

- Description of the Restaurant
- Background of the Restaurant
- The Company's Mission Statement
- The Unique Concept
- Location

Figure 4.1, Outline, *continued.*

- Restaurant Industry Trends
- Other Resources
- The Management
- Objectives and Financial Expectations
- Product and Service
- Pricing and Profitability
- Product Life Cycle
- Market Analysis
- Competition
- Customers
- Marketing Strategy
- Personnel
- Risk
- Loan Request and Anticipated Benefits
- Summary of Part One

Part Two: Financial Projections

- Start-Up Requirements
- Estimated Annual Sales
- List of Furniture, Fixtures and Equipment
- Leasehold Improvements
- Sources and Uses of Funds
- Income Statement for First Year
- Projected Income Statement—Month by Month
- Cash Flow Statement by Month
- Daily Breakeven Analysis
- Conclusion and Summary of Part Two

Part Three: Supporting Documents

(All legal and professional documents and any other applicable documents that will strengthen the plan.)

How To Construct a Business Plan

The Cover Page

The cover page tells the reader who they are dealing with. It should include:

- The legal name of your business and if your restaurant will be doing business under another name (DBA, or doing business as), that name as well
- The date the business plan is issued
- The name and title of the principal person submitting the plan
- The address and telephone number of the business

If you are submitting copies of the plan to several people or firms, you may wish to number each copy. The number should appear on the cover page.

The Table of Contents

The table of contents tells what is contained in the plan and where it appears. Page numbers should be inserted after the plan is completed in every other respect.

It is recommended that you number the pages using chapter and page numbers, such as 1.1, 1.2, 1.3. for Chapter 1, and 2.1, 2.2, 2.3 for Chapter 2, and so on. This allows you to add pages at the last minute without having to renumber the entire document.

For clarity and emphasis, always start new sections on a new page. Business plans will typically run 20 or more pages.

Statement of Purpose

The statement of purpose explains, in a summarized way, what the rest of the report covers in detail. Essentially, it answers the who, what, when, where and how much questions.

- Who is the report about? Who is asking for the loan?
- What is your legal form of ownership? (Sole-proprietorship, partnership, corporation, Subchapter S corporation.)
- How much funding is sought?

- What will the funds be used for?
- What benefits will accrue to the restaurant from the use of the funds?
- How will the borrowed funds be repaid? If you are seeking outside funding, this information will be of great interest to a lender. If you are preparing the business plan for your own use, it should be of equal interest for you to know the restaurant's potential for achieving your desired profit objective.

Part One: The Business

In this section, you will describe the business and tell what it will do, or sell, and how it will do it.

Description of the Restaurant. Tell its name, intended starting date, the kind of menu and style of service it will offer, its days and hours of operation, the names of the investors and their roles in the business.

Background of the Restaurant. Explain how the idea began, describe your research findings from surveys and interviews and indicate why the findings support your proposed business.

The Company's Mission Statement. Concisely state your overall goal for the restaurant, throughout its lifetime, as you now see it.

The Unique Concept. Explain the uniqueness of your restuarant. Describe it in detail, telling how it will fit into the marketplace. Focus on the desirability of your concept. Photographs and illustrations are useful in highlighting key items of interest. Lengthy exhibits should be placed in the appendix at the back of the document and referenced in the body of the text.

Location. Enumerate the reasons why you have chosen the proposed site and tell what its salient features are. This information can be obtained from your Property Analysis Checklist.

Restaurant Industry Trends. Cite predictions by restaurant industry analysts for the next year or two. Reference the sources from which information was obtained, such as the National Restaurant Association, your state hospitality association, the National Licensed

Beverage Association, the Bureau of Alcohol, Tobacco and Firearms, trade journals, census data, etc.

Other Resources. Financial: List your food and equipment suppliers and state their credit terms. Professional: List your lawyer, accountant, banker, insurance agent and consultants.

The Management. List your management team. Describe their personal histories, stating their training and experience in the restaurant field. Point out how they are suited to the duties and responsibilities they will be assuming. Their proposed salaries should be stipulated, as well as anything about them that will enhance the business's chances for success.

Objectives and Financial Expectations. Indicate your short-term and long-term goals for sales, customer acceptance, growth and expansion. Tell where you want the business to go—recount what you wish to achieve, stressing quality, profits, return on investment and public service. Your objectives should be feasible, understandable and realistic in terms of the resources you will have to work with.

Tell the benefits that investors and lenders may expect to realize when the restaurant's short- and long-term objectives are met. The point here is to convince potential investors or lenders that all aspects of the project have been carefully considered and that the idea makes sense. But be accurate and thorough because the business plan is first and foremost for your edification.

Product and Service. Tell what will differentiate your product and service from that of your competitors—explain what its benefits are. Here is where you inform the reader on how the restaurant will fill a market niche and how the menu and the style of service you offer are demanded by the target market. Stress the competitive advantages your restaurant will have. If your concept or product is based upon any proprietary secrets, such as recipes, you will want to protect them by asking prospective investors and lending institutions to sign a Nondisclosure Agreement.

Pricing and Profitability. Describe your pricing strategy and its profit generating potential. Explain how you set prices and their relationship to costs. Comment on the competitiveness of your prices. Relate the profit potential to the payback period for investors and lenders. Copies of menus, with prices, should be included in the appendix.

Product Life Cycle.   Tell what the expected life cycle is for your concept or product in the targeted marketing area. If your concept is one that has a high front-end acceptance, such as a trendy theme restaurant or a high-energy club, but has a limited life expectancy, point out the quick payback and lofty earnings potential.

Market Analysis.   This section describes your market as it currently exists—define it clearly. Include charts where applicable. Your explanation must leave no doubt in the investors' or lenders' minds that the proposed business is appropriate for the market.

Discuss any economic conditions or market changes that may be taking place. Tell how they will benefit the business. Indicate the size of the marketing area and its potential for future growth. Detail your strengths, and emphasize your marketing plans, as much as your product. Point out any unexploited opportunities you may recognize.

Be realistic and identify any weaknesses that you or the business may have and describe the ways you plan to eliminate or improve the weaknesses. This is a way to cope in advance with objections that an investor or lender might bring up.

Competition.   Identify your five or six nearest competitors. Elucidate the process by which you obtained information about your competitors to give your findings credibility. Tell what they offer, how they advertise (frequency, type of media used and size of advertisements). Show how that compares with what you plan to offer. Indicate what their strengths and weaknesses are and explain how your marketing strategy is designed to meet and overcome the competition.

Customers.   Give the demographics of your targeted clientele. Tell who your customers are, where they live, how educated they are, what income bracket they tend to be in, how they spend their money, what their wants and needs are as evidenced by research, what the motivation will be for them to patronize your establishment, what benefits they will receive from your restaurant, and why you can expect they will be attracted to it.

Marketing Strategy. This part of your business plan will guide you as you respond to business conditions and opportunities. It can make the difference between mediocrity or failure and the achievement of your goals. It should tell how you intend to position your restaurant (how your customers will perceive you) and how, by contrast, you can reposition your competitors (make your customers think of them). Likewise, it should detail the segment of the market you plan to reach and the share of the market you expect to capture.

Describe the selling and advertising tactics you will use to accomplish your goals. List your outside resources, advertising and public relations agencies, the media you will use and any sales promotional campaigns you intend to utilize. Tell who will be responsible for these areas.

Personnel. Describe your hours, days of business and your style of service. These factors will determine how many of each type of employee you will need and the skills required. An organizational chart accompanied by a proposed personnel schedule should be included here, along with estimated payroll costs.

Risk. Show in a convincing manner that you understand the risks of the restaurant business and have plans for managing them. These might include insurance programs, cost controls and specialized training for employees.

Loan Request and Anticipated Benefits. This section is used when seeking external funding. It should state the sum being applied for, contain an itemized list of the intended uses of the funds and a declaration of the benefits that will be realized from their utilization. The display of sources and uses of funds will be restated in the Financial Projections in Part Two.

Summary of Part One. The summary consists of a few paragraphs that capsulize the contents of Part One. They should tell who you are, what you want to do, how you plan to do it, when and where, what it will cost, why it is feasible, what the benefits are and (where applicable) how much you want to borrow.

Part Two: Financial Projections and Supporting Documents

The financial statements that compose Part Two of the business plan are illustrated in detail in the appendix.

The supporting documents section may include market survey data, drawings and layouts. It should include all legal and professional documents that support the information contained in Parts One and Two, as well as credit reports, letters of recommendation, letters of intent, copies of leases, contracts, personal resumes of all principals and their personal balance sheets, as well as any other documents that will strengthen the plan.

Action Guidelines

✔ Firm up the concept of your proposed restaurant and be able to describe it clearly.

✔ Talk to business brokers and real estate agents to determine economic conditions in the market areas in which you are interested.

✔ Conduct market research. Study your target market. Know the wants and needs of your prospective clientele.

✔ Evaluate the opportunities and the competition.

✔ Use the outline of a business plan in this chapter and the sample business plan in the appendix as a guide for writing your own business plan.

✔ Determine your financial needs.

✔ Present the business plan to prospective investors or institutional lenders (if desired), or use it for your own purposes as a management tool.

DEVELOPING MENUS THAT SELL

The menu influences everything in a restaurant. It must be perfectly matched in content and form with your sales objectives, the expectations of your customers, your style of service, the decor, your equipment and inventory.

Who Should Plan the Menu?

The planning of menus should be a cooperative effort between the chef and the manager. The chef knows the capabilities of the kitchen staff and the equipment, as well as the availability of food products and their cost. The manager, on the other hand, is largely concerned with sales objectives, profitability and image of the restaurant. Together, they cover all of the main concerns of a restaurant.

If a restaurant has a banquet department or a bar, it is wise to consult with the heads of those operations to determine any special needs of their clientele. Feedback may also be obtained from customer comment cards, where they are used.

Types of Menus

A variety of menus are utilized by restaurants—each has its appeal to a specific segment of the market. Once you know the wants and needs of your target market, you are ready to plan your menu. Following are the most common ones.

À la Carte Menu. Foods are listed separately and each item is individually priced.

Table d'Hôte Menu. A complete meal is offered for one all-inclusive price.

Du Jour Menu. The menu of the day, it is sometimes used for daily specials in conjunction with one of the other forms.

Limited Menu. This menu offers a limited number of entrees that do not change often.

Function Menu. It offers a group of specially designed complete meals or buffets from which function planners may choose for banquets.

Considerations When Developing a Menu

A menu should have balance, variety and an attractive composition. For example, an entree consisting of chicken à la king, mashed potatoes with light gravy, and cauliflower would be unappealing—it would have a pasty texture, monotonous colors, and lack distinctive tastes. The expression that people eat with their eyes has much truth; they are impressed by what they see. All menu items should appear and taste tantalizing to guests, regardless of their price. Following is a list of ways that a menu may be varied:

- Type of meat: beef, poultry, fish, pork
- Method of preparation: broiled, boiled, baked, fried
- Colors of the components on the plate: red, yellow, brown, white and green
- Textures of the items: crisp, tender, soft
- Shapes: flat, mounded, round, shredded, random
- Sizes of foods: all items should not be the same portion size
- Temperature of items: some items may be cold, such as salads
- Cost of entrees: offer a price range that appeals to all of your target market

Limitations on Your Menu

A number of questions should be asked as you plan your menu. Does it match your customers' expectations, or will they come to your restaurant expecting one thing and find another? This is where your market research will pay off.

Challenge each item as you consider it for inclusion in your menu. Is it available all year or just seasonally? Is it worth promoting for only a short period of availability? Some items are imported from other countries in the off-season, but their prices are considerably higher due to the expensive air transportation that has to be used. How would such price increases impact your menu?

Consider your staff—do your employees have the necessary skills to produce the item in a high-quality manner? Does the item require such intricate production skills that it would disrupt the pace of the kitchen staff whenever one was ordered?

Equipment must also be taken into account. You may have designed a great menu, but can you deliver it? Will the new item put additional pressure on equipment that may already be over-utilized? Is it worth buying another piece of equipment just to produce this item for your menu, and if it is, can it be installed where you want it?

This type of questioning must also be applied to your dining room staff and equipment. Suppose a restaurant wished to offer crêpes Suzette, prepared at tableside. This would require a gueridon cart, chafing dishes, a skilled waitperson capable of preparing the flamed delicacy safely and adequate aisle space to maneuver the cart throughout the dining room. Unless all of these conditions could be met feasibly, it would be unwise to include that item in the menu.

Format Is Important

Although no rigid rules exist, common sense dictates that menus should be easy for guests to handle while seated at a table and should be easy to read. The progression of items in the menu layout should be generally the same as that in which a guest would be apt to order—appetizers and salads first, followed by entrees and finally desserts. In addition, menus should not be cluttered or so long as to make selection difficult for the guest.

In the case of ethnic restaurants, unless it is certain that most customers will understand the language of the restaurant, it is wise to add English descriptions beneath foreign names. It speeds up ordering time and makes guests feel more comfortable.

Lighter foods or specialty items to which you may want to call attention may be listed separately. It is generally considered better to intersperse menu items, rather than list them in the precise order of their price—highest to lowest or lowest to highest. Mixing the items causes guests to focus less on the price and more on the qualities of an item.

Some restaurants will print everything but the prices on their menus, so that the menus will not have to be discarded whenever prices change. The practice of filling-in prices with a pen is more common in lower-priced establishments and those whose prices change frequently. It should be noted that unless the prices are written neatly in good handwriting, the menus will look messy. Prices should never be crossed out and have new ones written beside them.

Clip-ons featuring a new or special item may be attached to printed menus and if used tastefully they are not objectionable. However, they should be located carefully, so that they will not completely hide the items that they are placed over on the menu.

The materials that menus are made of vary widely—there is no end to the possibilities of what you may use, if you are creative. Some menus can be found on novelty materials such as wooden boards, leather aprons, miniature slateboards and even painted on walls and objects such as frying pans. The only caveat here is the physical menu should be appropriate to your decor, theme and style of service.

The most common menu materials are heavy paper or card stock, mainly because they are less expensive and easier to replace. Both of these materials should be coated to allow for cleaning when soiled or be inserted into protective covers. Menus should be inspected daily to remove any that are messy or dog-eared from service.

Attractive menu holders can be purchased in leather or plastic, and can be filled with changeable inserts. The advent of desktop computers and laser printers has made a wide variety of type faces and sizes available. Print-shop quality menus can now be produced in-house quickly and inexpensively, and best of all they can be changed as often as desired with a minimum of effort.

The typeface chosen for a menu is important because it can convey messages about a restaurant—formal elegance, casual simplicity—whatever is desired. The main thing to consider when selecting a typeface is readability. Some fonts, such as Old English, are attractive but difficult to read and are therefore best used sparingly. If your restaurant caters to significant numbers of senior citizens, you might consider using type of a larger point size.

"Truth in menus" must always be kept in mind when designing your menu. Today, people are much more concerned about what they eat than ever before and they are very sensitive to being misled by menus. You must be careful about how you use words like fresh, natural, homemade and light. Disgruntled guests may not complain, but they will tell others and will probably not return to your restaurant.

An interesting history of a restaurant, when printed on a menu, can provide entertaining reading for guests while they are waiting for service. If it is sufficiently interesting, it may also generate discussion and valuable word-of-mouth advertising with friends.

Children's Menus Sell Adult Dinners

The main reason for having children's menus is to attract adults. Parents want to enjoy themselves when they go to a restaurant and this can only happen when their children are happy.

Children's menus offer nothing more than adult foods offered in smaller portions, with a less formal presentation. For example, parents like to eat steaks, but children often prefer burgers (chopped steak).

With a little creativity, children's menus can be used to entertain them until their food arrives. The back side of a children's menu can be a connect-the-dots puzzle, a simple quiz or a coloring picture. Many things can be done to make dining with children a pleasant experience for parents. For example, some restaurants offer them a chance to reach into a treasure chest from which they can pull out an inexpensive novelty gift, if they clean their plates.

Many establishments specify that their children's menu applies only to youngsters up to age 12, when accompanied by a parent ordering from the regular menu. This is done to deter adults who want a small portion from ordering from the children's menu. However, if a restaurant has a significant number of customers that request smaller portions, it should consider adding a special light meal section to its regular menu. Children's menu items will often have a higher food cost percentage than adult menus, because they are considered a promotional item.

Standards Are Necessary

Customers want the assurance that every time they return to a restaurant and order their favorite dish, it will look the same and taste the same as it did the last time they ordered it. That assurance can only be achieved by having standards—standard recipes, standard portion sizes and standard methods of prepartion.

Few things will irritate a customer more than noticing that someone else with the same entree has received a larger portion or a better-looking product than they did. This tends to occur because cooks are inclined to vary recipes from day to day according to their mood. Having standard sizes and preparation methods for all items reduces the chances of that happening.

Menu Pricing—A Marketing Tool

The prices a restaurant charges influence the type of clientele it attracts. People of lower incomes usually patronize restaurants with economical prices, while people with higher incomes tend to patronize fancier restaurants. Higher prices are usually associated with superior service, elegant cuisine, a special location or entertainment.

Management should test its prices frequently to assure that they are appropriate to the style of service, the quality and quantity of the food served and are in line with those of comparable competitive establishments. At any level of pricing, customers must perceive that they are receiving value commensurate with the prices being charged. Few second chances are given in the food and beverage business, and people tend to be less forgiving of poor quality or service when they are charged higher prices.

Methods of Pricing a Menu

There are numerous ways to price menu items. Each has merit under certain circumstances but care should be taken to select the one that is most appropriate for your restaurant. In the end, any method you choose must produce prices that are sufficient to cover all of your costs and produce a profit.

It is important when calculating menu prices for a new restaurant that your estimated costs and desired profits be realistic. Industry statistics, available from the National Restaurant Association, for similar operations can be extremely useful when planning. Four common ways to set menu prices are shown below:

Method 1—Total Costs Plus Desired Profit

This method takes into account all of the costs of your restaurant as shown in your estimated income statement. It also considers the percentage of profit you desire to earn.

For example, if your estimated income statement revealed the following cost and profit percentages, and the raw food cost of the item you are pricing is $2.95, you can calculate its selling price by using the formula shown below:

<u>Estimated Income Statement Data</u>

All costs other than food cost   59.72%

Desired profit (on total sales)   10.00%

Formula:

$$\frac{\text{Food}}{\text{Cost \$}} + \frac{\text{All Other}}{\text{Costs \%}} + \frac{\text{Desired}}{\text{Profit \%}} = \text{Selling Price (100\%)}$$

Step 1: Calculate what your food cost percentage should be.

$2.95 + 59.72\% + 10\% = \text{Selling Price (100\%)}$

$2.95 + 69.7\% \qquad = \text{Selling Price (100\%)}$

$2.95 = 30.3\% \ (100\% - 69.7\% = 30.3\%)$

30.3% is your food cost percentage.

Step 2: Calculate the selling price of the item.

$$\frac{\$2.95}{.303} = \$9.74 \text{ Selling Price (round to \$9.75)}$$

Method 2—Percentage Markup on Cost

Once a meaningful food cost percentage has been developed as described in Method 1, it may continue to be used until any significant changes occur in the restaurant's costs.

To illustrate, assume that a new entree to be added to your menu has a raw food cost of $3.10. You could calculate its selling price simply by dividing the cost of the ingredients by the food cost percentage.

$$\frac{\text{Cost of ingredients}}{\text{Food cost percentage}} = \frac{\$3.10}{.303} = \$10.23 \text{ Selling Price (round to \$10.25)}$$

Unfortunately, some restaurants operate with an arbitrary food cost percentage, such as the often referred to 33.3 percent. This can be risky because the percentage has not been developed in relation to their other costs (as described in Method 1) and could be too high and result in a loss.

For example, suppose in the above example, it was arbitrarily decided to use a food cost percentage of 33.3 percent instead of the 30.3 percent developed by Method 1. A selling price of only $9.31 would have resulted (instead of $10.23). That means every entree sold would have been underpriced by 92 cents.

$$\frac{\text{Cost of ingredients}}{\text{Desired food cost percentage}} = \frac{\$3.10}{.333} = \$9.31 \text{ (Selling Price)}$$

The percentage method is easy to work with and is acceptable if the percentage used is one that was originally determined by an analysis of the actual costs of an operation, rather than an arbitrarily chosen one.

Method 3—Charging What the Market Will Bear

This method, often referred to as *skimming the market*, works best when you are the first one with a new concept that is in strong demand and you do not have any competition.

Essentially, it involves testing the market for the highest price that people are willing to pay and skimming the cream off the market until competitors come along and force you to lower your prices. For that reason, this is considered a short-term method of pricing.

It is essential, however, to be aware of your *pricing points*. Those are limits in consumers' minds—prices above which they do not perceive your products or services to be worth what you are charging.

Method 4—Competition Based Pricing

This refers to charging the same prices as your competitors do. This can be chancy because they may be more efficient or have greater purchasing power than you; consequently, you may not be able to produce a profit if you duplicate their prices. It is not a practice to be followed blindly but, rather, one that should be factored into your decision-making process when using the other methods.

Old-Fashioned Specials Still Draw People

Years ago most restaurants offered what was known as the "blue plate special." Actually, very few restaurants used blue plates, but the specials were popular because they were recognized as a good meal that usually sold at a lower price. Today, the term "specials" most often refers to items that are not printed on the menu and, by contrast to the blue plate specials, are not usually lower priced.

Some restaurants, however, still maintain the old concept and have built a base of loyal customers by offering specials of the day that are both good and favorably priced. An example of how a complete luncheon special could be priced is shown in Figure 5.1.

Will Your Restaurant Serve Alcoholic Beverages?

If you are going to serve alcoholic beverages, you will need to create wine lists or beverage menus. Much of what has been said about food menus applies to beverage menus as well—they must be attractive, easy to read, have variety, meet the expectations of the target market and be priced properly.

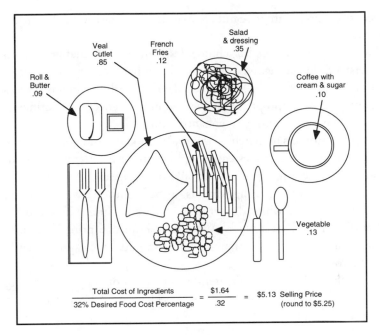

Figure 5.1: Illustrates how a complete luncheon special may be packaged and favorably priced to build sales volume.

How To Design a Wine List

Wines sell much better when they are promoted, and your wine list is your best sales promotion tool. A good wine list should have enough choices to be interesting and should complement your food menu, but it should not be so long as to be confusing.

The wines you carry should be consistent with your style of service and price structure. Small, modestly priced restaurants with a simple style of service may do well with lower-priced house wines, but an upscale restaurant will be expected to carry an extensive list of premium wines. It is good to search out new wines that your customers might enjoy, but be careful not to make your dining room a testing ground for new products.

Be sure to carry the items that are popular with your clientele. Check your wine inventory turnover periodically to weed out the slow movers—allowing of course for rarer wines that move slowly because of their high price but are maintained in stock for their prestige value.

When writing a wine list, choose descriptive words that are easy to understand. Avoid vague expressions, like "it has excellent nose and an extravagant taste that challenges the palate." Also shun snobbish words that may send inappropriate messages to inexperienced wine drinkers. Try to use positive words that enhance the appeal of your wines and assist your customers in matching them with food items. Operate on the premise that all your wines are good, but some are better with certain foods. If a wine is not good, you should not carry it.

A logical order for listing wines is (a) before-dinner wines, (b) red dinner wines, (c) white dinner wines, (d) sparkling wines and (e) after-dinner or dessert wines. Wine lists should be printed on substantial stock and your restaurant name should appear prominently on the cover page.

As with food menus, some items can be promoted by highlighting them with a different ink color or typeface, or by boxing them to draw attention.

Figure 5.2: A lobby display of wines stimulates interest as guests wait for tables at the Woods Restaurant in the New England Center, Durham, New Hampshire. (Photo by Bud Young. Courtesy of the New England Center.)

Pricing Alcoholic Beverages in General

As with food, the selling price of an alcoholic beverage must be adequate to cover all costs and produce a desired profit. The methods by which restaurant prices of wines, beer and mixed drinks are calculated vary because of the differences in the products themselves. Unlike food products, the selling price of alcoholic beverages, once calculated, may be further adjusted to compensate for high costs of liquor liability insurance, entertainment, free snacks and other expenses associated with beverage alcohol.

Pricing Wines

The philosophy for pricing wines has always been different than that of mixed drinks. Partly because wines are most often bought by the bottle and also because they are considered add-on sales. They are usually consumed during a meal and compete mainly with water, which is free. It is considered best to use a flexible markup system and sell a lot of wine, than to price wines with the high markups of liquors and sell much less.

Under the flexible markup system, higher cost wines are priced for resale with a smaller percentage of markup than lower cost wines. This makes finer wines more affordable and increases their sales.

Example:
  Wine A — Costs $10.50 per bottle.
           It is priced with a 100% markup to sell at $21.00.
           Gross profit per bottle = $10.50.
  Wine B — Costs $28 per bottle.
           It is priced with only a 50% markup to sell at $42.00.
           Gross profit per bottle = $14.00.

In the above example, the restaurant will earn an additional $3.50 of gross profit when they sell a bottle of wine B ($14.00 − $10.50 = $3.50). Even though a smaller percentage of markup was used for pricing wine B, it yielded a larger dollar amount of gross profit. Beside that, more customers will perceive wine B as being a relatively good value.

Pricing Beer

Three main factors determine the selling price of draught beer (pronounced "draft"). They are: the cost of the beer, the size of the beer glass used and the size of the head poured. In general, the selling prices of draught beer are calculated as follows:

Assume:	Half barrel keg costs	$48.00
	Keg contains	1980 ounces (approximately)
	Cost per ounce	$0.024
	Cost per 14-ounce goblet (which actually holds about 12.2 ounces of beer, assuming a one-inch head is poured)	$0.30
	Marked up five times, to accommodate a desired 20% pouring cost percentage	$1.48 Selling price (round to $1.50)

Following is an illustration of how to calculate the profit potential of a keg of beer (assume a one-inch head of foam is poured per glass).

Size of glass used	14 ounces
No. of glasses in a keg (half barrel)	162
Selling price per glass	$1.50
Total sales value of a half-barrel keg (162 × $1.50)	$243.00
Less: Cost of half-barrel keg	$48.00
Profit on a half-barrel keg	$195.00

In the above example, the restaurant is selling draught beer at a 20 percent pouring cost and yet its price is competitive. The four keys to selling a lot of beer are to (1) carry the brands your customers want, (2) keep your beer stored at the proper temperature (38° to 42° F.) and gauge pressure (12-14 psi), (3) keep your dispensing system meticulously clean and (4) price beer competitively.

Some brew-pub restaurants make their own beer. The recent popularity of premium micro-beers illustrates that many discriminating beer drinkers are willing to pay substantially more for a bottle of their favorite premium beer, provided they can take their time drinking it in a pleasant atmosphere.

Most full-service restaurants now carry at least one premium beer. The secret to selling a lot of premium beers is to know the brands your customers want and carry them. Although micro-beers cost more at wholesale, they command much higher prices at retail and can be very profitable.

Pricing Mixed Drinks

There are a number of approaches to pricing mixed drinks. All are acceptable as long as they cover costs and yield a desired profit. Following is one method for pricing drinks:

Assume:
a) A liter (33.8 oz.) of whiskey costs $9.40.
b) Drink prices are based on a 20% pouring cost (that means 20% of the price of a drink goes to pay for its ingredients).
c) Your standard pour is 1½ ounces (a pour is the amount of alcohol you put into a standard drink).
d) You allow 1.8 ounces, out of a liter bottle, for spillage. 33.8 oz.–1.8 oz. = 32 salable ounces or 21.3 pours of 1.5 oz. each.

Step 1:

Cost of Bottle	÷	Pouring Cost %	=	Sales Yield
$9.40	÷	.20	=	$47 (sales yield of bottle)

Step 2:

Sales Yield	÷	No. of Pours	=	Selling Price
$47	÷	21.3	=	$2.20 (unadjusted selling price)

Step 3:
Add a "kicker" of 25¢ to 50¢ to cover the cost of garnishes and mixers. The selling price may be further adjusted to defray entertainment costs, an unusually high rent or any other special considerations, such as high liquor liability insurance cost.

Using the above method, the example drink would probably sell for $2.75 to $3.25 or more. The same pricing system could be used for larger drinks and drinks requiring more liquors, by calculating the selling price of the additional liquor to arrive at a higher drink price.

Prior to the advent of computerized cash registers, restaurant owners were concerned that bartenders and servers would not be able to remember a great many prices and felt that mistakes would more than offset the benefits of pricing every drink individually. Consequently, a tiered pricing system was frequently used. Under the tiered system all drinks that were made with one liquor would have one average price, all two-liquor drinks would have another average price and so on for three-liquor drinks.

Today, computerized cash registers can be programmed to handle as many drink prices as a restaurant needs, and they are easy for bartenders to use. There is nothing to remember—the bartender simply presses the register key bearing the name of the drink and the computer finds the price of the drink in its memory. The register can tell the bartender how much change to give the customer, record the amount of liquor used and count the number of each type of drink served, hour by hour if you wish.

Action Guidelines

✔ Research your target market to determine their wants and needs.

✔ Visit other restaurants with a similar concept to examine their menus and style of service.

✔ Analyze the pros and cons of the various types of menus.

✔ Write an à la carte menu for your restaurant.

✔ Establish standard portions sizes for all items on your menu.

✔ Evaluate your menu for variety in the following areas and make adjustments as necessary:

- Type of meat used
- Methods of cookery
- Colors of foods on the plate
- Textures of the foods
- Tastes of the foods

✔ Develop food and beverage prices for your menus.

THE FRONT
OF THE HOUSE

The term *front of the house* refers to all of the service areas in a restaurant; it extends from the front entrance to the kitchen door. It is the customer contact point—where customers are won or lost. For that reason, all activities in the front of the house should be focused exclusively on satisfying customers.

Customers' perceptions of a restaurant are often set in the first few minutes of their visit by the promptness with which they are recognized, the smile of the person that greets them and the ambiance of the dining room. Benjamin Franklin once said, "The taste of the roast is often determined by the handshake of the host." No truer words could apply to the restaurant business.

Environment and Decor

Everything a customer sees, feels, smells or hears in your establishment is a part of its decor. The instant customers pull on your front door handle, they are experiencing your decor. A massive front door with heavy hardware conveys one image, while a small, lightweight door with economical hardware conveys a totally different image.

So it is with everything in your establishment—colors, sizes, shapes, weights and textures are all part of your decor and must be coordinated to produce the image you desire.

Your Message Must Be Clear

Customers should never be in doubt as to what your image message is. Everything about your establishment should contribute to the image you desire. The items listed below should be coordinated to project the same message:

1. Name of the business
2. Building design
3. Signs (colors, size, type of print)
4. Style of tables and chairs
5. Chinaware and flatware
6. Tablecloths and napkins

Figure 6.1: A dramatic view of the dining room of the Woods Restaurant at the New England Center, Durham, New Hampshire. (Photo courtesy of the New England Center.)

7. Carpeting or flooring

8. Wall hangings, pictures and drapes

9. Light fixtures

10. Menus (the physical menu)

11. Floor plan (table spacing)

12. Uniforms

13. Plants or other decorator objects

Aim to meet your patrons' expectations—define your target market before designing and decorating your restaurant. The wants and needs of your desired clientele should dictate the type and style of decor. With that clearly in mind, an appropriate theme should be developed and maintained throughout the front of the house.

Organization and Training

Good service doesn't just happen. To operate smoothly, the front of the house must be properly staffed with well-trained waitpeople. Factors that affect the staffing of a dining room are the style of service, the menu, hours of service and the size of the restaurant. Figure 6.2 depicts a typical dining room staff for a midsize, white tablecloth restaurant that serves lunch and dinner. Upscale restaurants may have additional ranks, such as captains and runners.

Normally, the host is in charge of the dining room. He or she is the person that greets guests as they arrive, takes their name, calls them when their table is ready, escorts them to their table, issues menus to them, monitors their table and thanks them on their way out. The host assigns a group of tables (called a wait station) to each waitperson and assigns parties of guests to the various stations throughout the shift. The pace of a dining room is set by the speed with which guests are seated by the host.

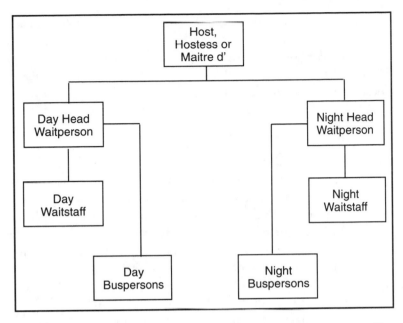

Figure 6.2: A typical organizational chart for a dining room staff in a full-service restaurant.

Allocating Space

Every style of service has its particular space requirements. Luxury dining implies large comfortable seating, more space per place setting and wider aisles than would be needed in lesser forms of service. The following space allocations are often referred to as a starting point when planning dining rooms:

Type of Dining	Sq. Ft. Per Person
Luxury dining	18 sq. ft.
Regular table service	15 sq. ft.
Cafeteria service	12 sq. ft.
Banquet service	10 sq. ft.

Additional space should be added for a lobby, coatroom, bus stations, restrooms and a lounge, where applicable. Salad bars and special decorator items in dining rooms, such as fountains and hearths, will also require additional space. For an example of a floor plan, see Figure 6.3.

Another consideration is the cost of square footage. In high-rent situations, tighter seating and a more judicious approach to space allocation may be used than where space is plentiful and less expensive.

Laying Out an Efficient Floor Plan

Your layout should appear friendly and inviting. It should excite your guests when they arrive and make them want to come again. To assure that guests get a pleasing view upon entering a restaurant, some free space, from which they can orient themselves and absorb the atmosphere, should be provided near the entrance.

If a restaurant has a lounge, it should be conveniently located so that bar customers will not have to walk through the dining room to get to it. The ideal location for a lounge is near the front entrance, where the host can easily reach people waiting for tables.

The physical layout of a dining room will have a direct relationship to its profitability. Waiters and waitresses must be able to move quickly as they take orders and deliver food and beverages—tight aisles and poor table arrangements can slow down service, irritate guests and reduce sales. Following are minimum recommended aisle widths that allow customers and servers to approach and leave their tables with relative ease:

Type of Aisle	Minimum Width Recommended
Main Traffic Aisle (from host's stand through dining room)	54"
Access Aisles (from main traffic aisle to wait stations)	36"
Service Aisles (space around tables)	18"–24"

If you plan to have a salad bar, a number of questions should be asked when allocating space for it. When and how often will it have to be stocked? From where will the supplies come? Will guest service be affected at those times? Will it impede the flow of traffic? The answers to these questions will influence the location of the aisles and the salad bar.

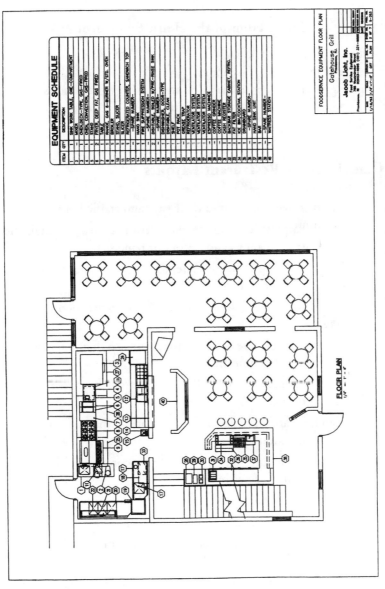

Figure 6.3: The floor plan of the Gatehouse Grill, in Providence, Rhode Island, is an example of an attractive and efficient restaurant layout. (Drawing courtesy of Jacob Licht, Inc., Providence, Rhode Island.)

Shown below is a list of front-of-the-house equipment items that are common to most full-service restaurants:

Typical Front-of-the-House Equipment

Tables	Chairs	Booths
Service Stands	Bus Stands	High Chairs
Cash Register	Cashier Counter	Coat Racks
Telephones	Restroom Fixtures	Banquettes
Lobby seats	Host Stand	

Guidelines for Restaurant Layouts

1. Avoid congestion around doorways and traffic lanes.
2. Divide large spaces into smaller, intimate areas through the use of walls, planters and decorator panels.
3. Use contrasting colors or materials to give smaller areas an atmosphere of their own.
4. Provide adequate aisles for waitstaff to deliver food and beverages.
5. Vary your table sizes and arrangements, so that you can handle parties of various sizes.
6. Folding doors may be used to create private rooms or to close off empty areas.
7. Plan food and beverage pickup stations so that they create the least distraction to guests.
8. Install intercom systems to facilitate communications with banquet and bar personnel.
9. Fire exits and safety equipment should be easily seen.
10. Provide adequate restroom facilities.
11. Restroom signs should be visible from most points in the restaurant.
12. In colder climates, ample facilities for coat hanging should be provided.
13. Choose easily cleanable materials for floors, walls and furniture.

How To Select Table Sizes

It is important to have adequate table sizes to match the needs of your clientele. If a party of two must be seated at a table for four because there are too few small tables, the extra two seats will be wasted. Similarly, if a party of five or six people has to wait an unusually long time for seating because a restaurant does not have larger tables, they will be annoyed. To avoid these problems, it is essential to have an appropriate variety of table sizes to meet the needs of your clientele. Figure 6.4 illustrates a method for calculating your table needs. In this example it is assumed the restaurant seats 150 and the expected makeup of the clientele is: parties of one or two people—20 percent, three or four people—50 percent and five or six people—30 percent.

Figure 6.4: Calculating Table Needs

Type of Table	Percent of Total Clientele		Total Seating Capacity		No. of Seats Needed		No. of Seats at Table		No. of Tables Needed
Tables for 2	20%	×	150	=	30	÷	2	=	15
Tables for 4	50%	×	150	=	75	÷	4	=	19
Tables for 6	30%	×	150	=	45	÷	6	=	8

In Figure 6.4, 15 tables for two, 19 tables for four and 8 tables for six would best accommodate the expected clientele.

Designing a Dining Room Service System

The easiest way to design a service system is to put yourself in your customer's shoes and walk through the process of entering a restaurant, being greeted and seated, and having your order taken and served. Then put yourself in an employee's shoes and walk through the process of greeting the customer, taking their order, turning it in to the kitchen, then picking it up and delivering it to the customer. In your mind's eye, you will envision every step of the service system from order-taking to cashiering.

Answering the following questions will assist in the process of planning a service system:

- How will guests arrive? As pairs, singles or as larger groups?
- What types of seating will you need?
- Will guests arrive by car? If so, do you have adequate and safe parking available?
- Where will guests enter and how will they be greeted? By whom? When? Where?
- Will your lounge be used to accommodate guests while waiting to be seated in the dining room?
- Where will your lounge be located, in relation to the main entrance and to the dining room?
- How will the waiting guests be called when their dining room table is ready?
- Will the lounge check be transferred to the dining room or must guests pay for their drinks before leaving the lounge?
- Will your dining room have smoking and nonsmoking areas? How large will each area be?
- Who will take the guests' cocktail order and dinner order?
- What kind of uniforms will your waitstaff wear?
- How will the food orders be delivered to the kitchen? Electronically? Verbally? Written?
- How will servers know when their orders are ready to be picked up?
- Who will set up and bus tables?
- Who will correct mistakes and void guest check items?
- Who will handle any complaints that might arise?
- How will the guest check be presented to the guest?
- Who will cashier the guest check?
- Where will charge card sales be written up?
- Will there be a coatroom for guests' wraps? Free? Coin operated? Coat checks?
- Where will your restrooms be located?
- Where will your telephones be located?

The Buddy System

To assure better service, the host will keep track of the parties that are seated at each station. This helps to prevent overburdening any one station. Still, overload situations occur on occasion. To alleviate such dilemmas, waitpersons should practice the *buddy system*, which simply means in an emergency, waitpeople will assist the station on either side of their station. In Figure 6.5 the waitperson in Station 2 is the buddy of the waitperson in Stations 1 and 3, and will assist those people in times of special need. They in turn will reciprocate when needed.

The head waitperson supervises the *side work*, which includes the preliminary setup of the dining room and the changeover between meal periods. A variety of tasks, ranging from filling salt and pepper shakers to folding napkins, must be done in order to make the dining room ready for guests. The head waitperson also makes up the dining room work schedules.

Depending upon the hours of service, waitpeople may work one or two meal periods straight through—such as breakfast and lunch. In the case of lunch and dinner, they will sometimes work a split shift because of the length of time between the two meals. The scheduling of employees is largely an accommodation between the restaurant and the individual. Some restaurants have found that utilizing flexi-

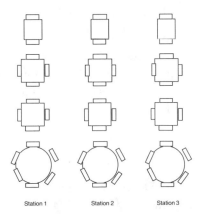

Station 1   Station 2   Station 3

Fig. 6.5: Typical waitstations in full-service restaurants will have about 16 seats.

ble schedules and working closely with their employees when scheduling hours serves both parties well.

Taking the Order

Waitpeople must be salespeople and ambassadors of goodwill because they are in the position of greatest contact with customers. As such they must be alert to customers' needs and respond with ingenuity when things go wrong. A skilled waitperson can often salvage a bad situation by simply displaying a pleasant and caring attitude.

A traditional way to take guests orders is to call upon ladies first, followed by elders, then children and finally men, moving counterclockwise around the table.

Abbreviations Reduce Chaos

Using standard abbreviations on guest checks speeds up the order taking process. More important however, abbreviations are very helpful to cooks and bartenders because they are consistent and easy to read.

Although there are no universal abbreviations, some make more sense than others. You can make up your own as long as everyone understands them and uses them consistently.

Here are some examples of abbreviations for food and drink items:

Food Abbreviations

Bk Chk /OB / Asp =	Baked Chicken with O'Brien potatoes and asparagus
Veal Salt / Sp Fet =	Veal Saltimbocca with spinach fettucini
Mx Gr / OR /FF =	Mixed Grill with onion rings and French fries

Drink Abbreviations

V Mart r tw =	a Vodka Martini, on the rocks, with a lemon twist
Sing Sling =	a Singapore Sling
Bour Man ↑ =	a Bourbon Manhattan, straight up

Customer Service

No matter how well employees are trained and systems are improved, service will deteriorate if it is not monitored constantly. Undesirable conditions should not be allowed to continue to the point that a customer has to complain, because by that time other customers who did not bother to register their displeasure will undoubtedly have already left your clientele. Management should be the first to know when things are not right. Following is a list of common situations that disturb customers:

- When a restaurant opens late or closes early
- When a guest is greeted impatiently, rather than with a smile
- When empty tables, in view of waiting guests, are not bused quickly
- When the restaurant floor, tables or chairs are not clean
- When tablecloths have holes or tears
- When menus are tattered or smudged
- When glasses or tableware are chipped
- When flatware is spotted, or coffee cups are stained
- When guests have to wait to place their drink or food order
- When guests see their food sitting on the serving line waiting to be picked up
- When beer or carbonated drinks arrive flat
- When baked items are stale or salads are limp
- When restaurants run out of advertised items prematurely
- When a waitperson does not know who ordered an item
- When a waitperson disappears for long periods of time
- When salads are not chilled and hot foods are barely warm when delivered
- When water glasses are not refilled
- When a guest check has been handled with greasy fingers
- When no one says, "Thank you for your patronage"

Designing Your Bar

In most full-service restaurants, the lounge is an integral and important part of the front of the house and as such, its theme and decor should be compatible with that of the restaurant.

Two basic questions must be answered when designing a bar, What types of beverages will be served? and How many customers will have to be served at one time? The answer to those two questions will form the basis of any bar layout.

The types of beverages that will be served will dictate what equipment is required, the styles of glasses needed, what is needed to prepare specialty drinks (ice cream, coffee, slush), the amount of refrigerated storage needed and whether to dispense draught beer or serve bottled beer.

The number of customers to be served will determine the quantity and size of the equipment, the amount of ice required, the number of glasses needed, how much glass storage space is necessary and how many serving stations are required. And since every drink begins with a clean, sterile glass, appropriate glass washing equipment is necessary.

After equipment sizes and quantities have been determined, the equipment has to be arranged to conform to the flow of the beverages and glasses to and from the serving stations. A *serving station* is the area and equipment used by a bartender to mix and dispense the variety of beverages required. A small restaurant bar can have a single serving station, staffed by one server, while a large bar may have several. The greater the number of customers to be served, the larger the bar and the more stations that are required for efficient operation.

It is important to think of a bar in terms of efficiency. How can a beverage order be prepared with the fewest number of steps? Where should the cocktail mixing station be in relation to the beer dispensing stations and in relation to the cash register? Will any specialty drinks have to be prepared and what is needed for them? How much floor space in relation to total space available can be dedicated to the bar operation? What is the budget? Will equipment cutbacks be necessary in order to meet budget constraints?

When a bar designer thinks about efficiency, uses common sense and "acts out" the workings of the operation, it will become clear in the planning stage what equipment is required and where it should be placed. In essence a good bar layout is no different than an efficient kitchen or office layout.

List of Typical Bar Equipment

Sinks, 3 compartment	Ice Chest with Cold Plate
Drainboards	Bottle Wells
Speed Racks	Ice Cube Maker
Overhead Glass Rack	Ice Crusher or Flaker
Glass Chiller	Glass Washer
Beer Tap	Glass Storage Rack
Beer Mug Froster	Liquor Display Shelves
Keg Beer Cooler	Back Bar Liquor Storage Cabinets
Bottled Beer Cooler	Speed Gun Soda System
Cash Register	Cocktail Stations
Ice Cream Cabinet	Condiment Trays
Work Boards	Blender Station

Some restaurants have *service bars* in the back of the house that make drinks for dining room guests only. They do not handle cash or wait on customers—the drinks are ordered and picked up by the wait-staff. Consequently, service bars need only a minimum of essential production equipment.

Action Guidelines

✔ Decide on a style of service for your restaurant.

✔ Choose a theme for your decor.

✔ Analyze your clientele, when they will arrive, numbers in party, etc.

✔ Determine your desired seating capacity.

✔ Layout a front-of-the-house floor plan.

✔ Design a service system for your restaurant.

✔ Make a list of the equipment that will be needed in the front of the house.

Chapter

7

THE BACK
OF THE HOUSE

The *back of the house* encompasses all of the production-related areas of a restaurant, from the receiving door in the back of the building to the dining room doors. When the back of the house runs smoothly, customers are happy in the front of the house, and that is the way you would like your kitchen to run all of the time.

A key contributor to a smooth-running kitchen is a good layout—and the easiest time to design one is before you open for business. It is always more difficult to make changes when you have equipment in place and are functioning. Kitchen renovations are both costly and time consuming, consequently many restaurants live with inconveniences for years, rather than disrupt their operations.

Analyze Your Needs

Your equipment will be determined by your menu. Every item should be analyzed in terms of what will be needed to prepare it. The equipment should then be arranged in a configuration that moves products steadily from the rear of the kitchen toward the dining room, with a minimum of backtracking and crisscrossing. All of your planning decisions should be focused on delivering the best product to your clientele in the shortest amount of time possible.

Allocating Kitchen Space

The amount of kitchen space needed to produce your menu will depend upon the extent to which you use convenience foods. Restaurants that make extensive use of convenience foods require much less equipment and work space than do restaurants that cook almost entirely from scratch. In the latter case, most products must be refrigerated, washed, prepared and processed, and that requires space, equipment and labor. The following relationships can serve as a starting point when planning a kitchen:

Extent to Which Convenience Foods Used	Approximate Size of Kitchen as Related to Dining Room
Little or no use of convenience foods	50%
Moderate use of convenience foods	40%
Extensive use of convenience foods	33⅓%

Additional space would be added for storerooms, locker rooms, trash rooms, employee restrooms and such other ancillary facilities as might be desired.

Working with Vendors

Many equipment vendors are qualified and willing to help businesses calculate their needs and layout a facility, for a fee. They have expertise and are acquainted with the latest foodservice products on the market. Moreover, you can benefit from the experience they bring from other projects. If your funds are tight, they can help you work within budget by suggesting alternatives.

In order for vendors to work successfully with you, however, they must have exact data regarding the size and shape of the rooms involved, the utilities available and the menu you will be producing.

On large or complex projects an architect who specializes in restaurant design should be engaged to build your facility. The architect, will in turn engage a food equipment consultant and subcontractors for each of the specialized areas of the project.

When selecting vendors, contractors or architects, ask for a list of their previous clients and check their references carefully to determine how satisfied the previous clients are.

Selecting Equipment

Your budget will influence the type, size and quantity of equipment you will select (see Figure 7.1 for picture of state-of-the-art equipment), but purchases of equipment should be made mainly on the basis of how you answer the following questions:

1. Is it essential to your operation? Will it improve your production or service systems?

2. Is it the right size? Will it do the job you expect of it in terms of volume, speed and quality?

3. Does the equipment bear the appropriate NSF, AGA, UL or ASME approval seals? Is it safe and sanitary?

4. Will it blend in well with the rest of your equipment? Does it have a good appearance?

5. Can it be serviced easily, and what type of warrantee does the seller or manufacturer offer?

6. Will it fit in the space you have available for it?

7. How much will the utility hookups and installation cost? Do you have the required water pressure, electrical phase and voltage?

8. Is it cost-effective in relation to alternative ways of getting the job done?

The Production System

A commercial kitchen is made up of a number of work centers that together comprise a *production system*. A good production system will flow steadily in one direction. The direction may be linear, circular or "m" shaped to fit a limited space, but it should always end up at or near the point of service. Typical work centers in a restaurant kitchen are the following:

- Receiving and storing
- Pre-preparation and salad making
- Sandwich and cold food preparation
- Cooking and serving
- Baking
- Dish washing and pot washing

Figure 7.1: A battery of modular cooking equipment, designed for easy cleaning and attractive appearance. (Photo courtesy of Market Forge Industries, Inc. of Everett, Massachusetts.)

Analyzing Equipment Needs

A chart similar to Figure 7.2 can be constructed to identify equipment needed to produce the menu. Only major equipment need be considered in this analysis.

Figure 7.2:

Equipment Analysis

Menu Item	Method of Preparation	Equipment Necessary
Homemade Soups	Stockpot cooking	Range Work table Refrigerator
Salads	Fresh	Refrigerator Work table Sink Disposer
Fried Chicken	Deep fried	Deep Fryer
Steaks	Broiled	Broiler
Hamburgers	Grilled	Griddle
Ham Steak	Baked	Conventional Oven
Baked Potatoes	Baked	Convection Oven

It is helpful to mentally visualize the process by which each item is made, from the starting point where its ingredients are gathered to the point where the product is cooked and served.

Work Center Layout

A *work center* is one section of a production system that is devoted to a particular function, such as baking, salad-making, cooking and dish-washing. Each center must be designed to perform its function efficiently and to interface smoothly with the other centers.

Three key issues should be considered when planning a work center: (1) what is the intended purpose of the work center, (2) what equipment will be needed to accomplish the intended purpose and (3) what are the spacial needs of the employees who will work in the center?

The first step in the process is to define the primary functions of the center. The second is to break down the the functions into the tasks required to accomplish them. Finally, the equipment needed to perform the tasks must be identified and laid out in a logical arrangement, with adequate space for employees to do their jobs safely and efficiently. Figure 7.3, on page 92, illustrates how a bakery work center might be designed.

How To Size Equipment

The sizing of equipment is done by calculating the volume of output you will require to satisfy your peak periods of business and finding a model that will produce the desired volume of output.

Be aware that on some types of equipment such as dishwashers, the capacities stated in manufacturers' catalogs are determined under the most ideal circumstances possible. To compensate for that, it is wise to reduce the manufacturers' claimed capacity by 30 percent when matching with your needs. The following example illustrates the steps that might be followed when selecting a conveyer type dishwasher.

1. Determine the average number of pieces of chinaware used per patron in your restaurant.

2. Estimate the total number of patrons you will serve in a peak hour, and multiply that number by the average number of pieces of chinaware used per patron.

$$\frac{No.\ of}{Customers} \times \frac{Avg.\ No.\ of\ Pcs}{of\ Chinaware} = \frac{Total\ No.\ of\ Pieces}{of\ Chinaware}$$

3. Divide the total number of pieces of chinaware by the number of pieces that will fit into a dish rack, for example, 20.

$$\frac{Total\ No.\ of\ Pcs.\ of\ Chinaware}{20} = \frac{No.\ of\ Racks\ Required}{Per\ Hour}$$

4. Refer to dish machine specifications in equipment catalogs and find a model that matches your desired capacity for a peak hour.

Figure 7.3:

Example: Laying Out a Bake Shop Work Center

Step 1: List the main functions of the bake shop: To bake breads, pies, cakes and other pastries.

Step 2: Break down the tasks required to perform functions and identify the equipment needed:

Tasks	Equipment Needed
Gather ingredients	Dry storage and refrigerator
Weighing	Baker's table and scale
Mixing	Mixer and sink with water hose
Kneading	Work table
Panning	Work table
Cook fillings and icings	Trunion kettle
Proofing	Proof boxes
Baking	Deck ovens
Landing and cooling	Work table and ladder rack carts
Slicing	Bread slicing machine
Decorating	Work table
Storage and delivery	Ladder rack carts

Step 3: Lay out the equipment in a functional manner.

1. Refrigerator
2. Mixer
3. Baker's Table
4. Sinker w/spray arm
5. S/S Worktables
6. Steam Jacketed Kettle
7. Proof Boxes
8. Deck Ovens
9. Ladder Rack Carts
10. Bread Slicer and Table
11. Decorating Table
12. Delivery Cart

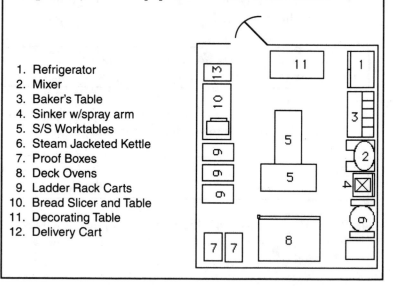

Should You Buy or Lease Equipment?

There are valid reasons for leasing and for buying equipment, but the reasons will vary from business to business and from time to time, due to fluctuating interest rates and alternative uses of funds.

Although there is not a single answer for all cases, it is important to understand the advantages and disadvantages of each course of action under varying circumstances. The pros and cons of buying and leasing are listed in Figure 7.4.

Figure 7.4:

Pros and Cons of Buying and Leasing
Buying

Advantages	Disadvantages
Buyer accumulates a valuable asset.	Equipment will wear out and need to be replaced by the buyer, eventually.
Buyer can depreciate a portion of the cost each year,	Buyer assumes the responsibility of maintaining and servicing the equipment.
Interest expense for installment payments is tax deductible.	

Leasing

Advantages	Disadvantages
Lease payments are tax deductible as business operating expenses.	Loss of depreciation write-off.
Lessor may maintain and service the equipment for the lessee.	At end of the lease you do not own the equipment.
Service calls on leased equipment are usually given priority over others.	The built-in charge for service may be more than you would otherwise have paid for it.
Lessor usually supplies brand new models, and updates equipment periodically.	

Perhaps the most important realization when considering leasing equipment is that old adage, Nothing is free. Everything you lease has a price that includes all expenses, plus a profit for the lessor. The main reason many people lease equipment is they just don't have the money to buy it.

Another reason for at least considering leasing is that it is a way to hedge if a new business is uncertain of its future. Assuming a short-term lease is entered, the lessee can terminate business with minimal losses, as opposed to a business that buys everything and gets stuck with a lot of money tied up in used equipment. It should be noted that used food and beverage equipment is plentiful and brings very little money at auction.

Typical Back-of-the-House Equipment

Range	Three Compartment Sink
Gas Broiler	Scale
Charcoal Broiler	Peeler
Deep Fat Fryer	Tilting Skillet
Roast Oven	Ladder Rack Carts
Steam Kettle	Proofing Cabinet
Compartment Steamer	Soiled Dish Table
Hoods and Vent	Dish Washer
Work Tables	Clean Dish Table
Bain Marie	Hand Sink
Griddle	Time Clock
Grill	Waste Disposal
Toaster	Dish Heater
Reach-in Refrigerator	Meat Grinder
Reach-in Freezer	Tenderizer
Pot and Pan Racks	Breading Table
Slicer	Pot Sink
Mixer	Desk
Attachment Rack	File Cabinet
Tenderizer	Computer

Efficiency Must Be Planned

When designing your floor plan, the efficiency of your operations must also be considered. Products should flow in a steady direction from receiving to the serving line. The flow of foot traffic should also be smooth and free of dangerous crisscrossing at busy intersections. Aisles must be wide enough for workers to perform their duties freely and to safely pass each other with hot or heavy pans:

Type of Kitchen Aisle	Minimum Width Recommended
Main Aisles (through kitchen)	72"
Work Aisles (between equipment)	48"

Additional space must be allowed near hazardous equipment, such as slicing machines and hot ovens with doors that swing into aisles.

Selecting Chinaware and Glassware

There are many types of ware to choose from—some work better with certain kinds of food and decor than do others. Five main features to look at when selecting tableware are:

1. Style
2. Size
3. Strength
4. Usefulness
5. Cost

Table settings are a key part of a restaurant's decor; therefore, the style should be based on your desired image and the kind of food you will be serving. Tableware should be easy to clean and should coordinate well with the overall decor of the restaurant. Plate sizes should be appropriate for the portions you plan to serve and that, of course, will be related to the prices you plan to charge. The strength and chip-resistence of chinaware and glassware is important. Vitrified china and chip-resistant glassware are made especially for the hotel and restaurant trade—they will cost more at the outset but will save you money over the long run.

How Much Should You Buy?

This will depend upon your estimated sales volume. Keep in mind that some items will be in use at tables, while others will be soiled and waiting to be washed. You should have a large enough reserve inventory of chinaware and glassware to handle all contingencies. Many establishments will keep a 25 percent reserve stock to be used for breakage replacements and very busy occasions. Once tableware is chipped, no matter how slightly, it must be removed from service.

Think carefully before ordering chinaware monogrammed with your name or initials on it. Even though it may be very appealing to the ego, it costs more money when you buy it, it requires a long lead time for delivery because it has to be specially made for you, dealers will not keep it in stock and unless someone else wants to use your name or has your initials, it is virtually worthless for resale.

Action Guidelines

✔ List the work centers that will be necessary to produce your menu.

✔ Determine the main function of each work center and determine tasks that need to be performed.

✔ Identify the equipment needed to perform the tasks.

✔ Develop a floor plan for each work center and design your kitchen by arranging the work centers in an efficient layout.

OPERATING PROFITABLY

To operate a restaurant profitably, you must keep a tight control over all of its profit centers. A *profit center* is an activity that, by its efficiency or inefficiency, can increase or decrease the profits of an operation. Typically, there are nine profit centers in a restaurant. They are:

1. Menu Planning
2. Purchasing
3. Receiving
4. Storing
5. Issuing
6. Pre-preparation
7. Cooking and production
8. Serving
9. Cashiering

Since the menu of a restaurant is the hub around which everything else revolves, it is essential to plan it carefully. The cross utilization of ingredients among a number of menu items should be planned so as to minimize the size of the inventory that must be carried to support your menu. Leftovers should also be given careful thought—wherever possible, a secondary application should be planned for every item on the menu. For example, one day's leftover roast pork could go into the next day's American chop suey.

Purchasing the right products in the proper quantities is important; and of equal importance is keeping them securely stored until they are used. Food and beverages are tempting products that may be easily pilfered if not adequately controlled. In a small restaurant where the boss or a supervisor is always present, it is not necessary to have the level of controls that are required in a larger restaurant where, because of the size of the operation, things are not always under the watchful eye of the manager. In large restaurants, where a formal food cost control program is maintained, products should be logged into an inventory book as soon as they are put away. The storeroom should be kept locked and withdrawals should be made only upon proper authority and should be recorded in the inventory book.

Waste can be reduced significantly, in the pre-preparation and cooking stages, by instituting certain *standards*. An example of a standard might be to cut eight slices or wedges out of every tomato, or it might be a standard recipe that specifies all of the ingredients and a step-by-step method for producing a menu item. When followed carefully, standard recipes insure a consistent taste and portion size for all menu items.

Finally, to close the control loop, all moneys collected should be accounted for. The cashier's copies of guest checks that were rung up during a shift should match the kitchen's duplicate copies of the guest checks, and the total of the guest checks should agree with the money in the cash register drawer.

Guest checks should be serially numbered and kept locked until they are issued to a wait person. They should always be used in consecutive order, and any missing checks should be accounted for by the wait person at the end of the shift during which they were lost.

Purchasing Wisely

Purchasing dollars are high-powered dollars because they flow right down to the profit line of a business. For instance, if a restaurant is netting 10 percent profit on sales, before taxes, it will take ten dollars of additional sales to make up for every dollar of profit lost through poor purchasing.

Wise purchasing not only involves buying at the right price, it includes buying the right quantities and grades and making sure you receive what you ordered. Slow moving items should be avoided because money tied up on storeroom shelves gathers dust, not interest, and a restaurant cannot afford to carry dead stock.

Inventory Turnover Rate

It is important to know how your inventory is moving—does it turn over once a week, once a month or longer? It is imperative to rotate your stock and to turn it over as frequently as possible because few products improve with age. Following are some reasons why slow moving or dead stock occurs:

1. Too much of a product was purchased.
2. Ingredients were bought for a product that did not sell well and were never used again.
3. Inventory is not taken regularly and dead stock goes unnoticed until it spoils.
4. A system of "forced issues," which requires the chef to use up old items, is not practiced.

There are instances when a low turnover rate of an item is intentionally tolerated, such as when fine wines are carried in inventory for their prestige value on the menu. In spite of this, a high degree of inventory control can still be maintained by simply removing those items from the calculations and focusing on the vast majority of the stock that should turn over rapidly.

Your *inventory turnover rate* is an indicator of how long it takes you to sell the goods that you buy. Put another way, it is the number of times your inventory is turned into cash, within a given period of time. The period of time can be whatever you wish—a month, a season or a year. A three-step method for calculating an inventory turnover rate is illustrated in the following example:

Step 1: Calculate the cost of the food consumed.

Beginning Food Inventory 1/1/9–	$ 4,000
Plus: Food Purchases 1/1–1/31	12,000
Total Food Available	$16,000
Less: Ending Food Inventory 1/31/9–	3,800
Cost of Food Consumed	**$12,200**

Step 2: Calculate the average food inventory.

Beginning Food Inventory 1/1/9–	$4,000

Plus: Ending Food Inventory 1/31/9–   3,800
Total (divide by 2 to get average) $7,800

$$\frac{\$7,800}{2} = \$3,900 \text{ Average Food Inventory}$$

Step 3: Calculate the inventory turnover rate.

$$\frac{\text{Cost of Food Consumed}}{\text{Average Food Inventory}} = \text{Food Inventory Turnover Rate}$$

$$\frac{\$12,200}{\$3,900} = 3.13 \text{ times}$$

In the preceding example, the food inventory was turned over about three times a month, or every nine and half days. Turnover rates may vary throughout the year, particularly for seasonal businesses. The optimum rate is the highest number of turnovers you can achieve that still allows you to cover your needs adequately between reorders and gives you a safety margin for emergencies and unexpected increases in sales volume.

Planning Your Initial Inventory

The size of your initial inventory will be based on several factors— the *frequency* with which you plan to reorder, the amount of *storage space* you have (dry storeroom, refrigerator space and freezer space), your *expected sales* volume and the amount of *money* you can afford to tie up in inventory. The inventory of most full-service restaurants is made up of five categories of products. They are:

- Meats, fish and poultry
- Fresh fruits and vegetables
- Dairy products
- Bakery products
- Groceries (canned, jarred and packaged products)
- Beverages

Some restaurants buy meats and poultry from one purveyor, while others have specialized purveyors for each type of item. Some meat companies distribute frozen seafood products, but, as a rule, fresh fish are sold by specialized vendors. Who you buy from is largely a matter of the availability of vendors and the quantities in which you buy.

Nonalcoholic beverages are purchased directly from soft drink bottlers, and alcoholic beverages are purchased from liquor companies in open states and from state liquor stores or warehouses in control states.

Your initial inventory should be based on the production needs of your menu. Care should be taken to avoid stocking many items that have only a one-time use, and when that happens, a plan for using up the leftover quantities should be instituted. The practice of making a chef find a use for the product within a certain period of time, is called *forced issues,* as discussed in Chapter 5.

After you have been in operation for a while, you can establish reliable maximum and minimum inventory levels for all items, based on their actual sales history. But, until sales trends develop, you will have to work from estimates.

Most vendors will work closely with new restaurants during their start-up period and will stock them properly. However, an overzealous salesperson will occasionally overload an account by offering a deal or a volume discount. There is little point in buying more than you need simply to obtain a discount if you have a tight budget or an alternative use for the money that might yield a greater return.

How To Buy Right

The goal of inventory management is to carry the products that are needed to produce your menu and keep your customers happy while not tying up your money needlessly. Establishments with a limited menu have a much easier task of selecting their initial inventory than do restaurants with an extensive menu. But even in the case of the extensive menu, over 80 percent of the items in inventory are constant.

Competitive buying is practiced by many restaurants. This entails telephoning two or three vendors early in the morning to get current market prices on items needed for that day and recording them on a quotation sheet (see Figure 8.1, on page 102). When all of the desired price quotations have been obtained, the restaurant calls back the vendors that it has decided to buy from and places its orders.

The practice of buying solely because of a low price is referred to as *cherry picking*. Most buyers will cherry pick some items, but will choose others on the basis of the vendor's dependability and level of service, or product characteristics aside from price.

It is recommended that restaurants keep some sort of written record of items ordered from distributors—such as a copy of the purchase order shown in Figure 8.2—because the person who receives shipments is not usually the person that placed the order. This allows

ON HAND	ITEM	QUANTITY WANTED	TELEPHONE QUOTES		
			VENDOR	VENDOR	VENDOR

The Branding Iron Steak House, Inc.
Daily Market Quotation Sheet
Date: _____

Figure 8.1: A sample market quotation sheet.

the receiver to compare the items shipped with the list of the items ordered and helps to quickly spot substitutions or incorrect items. It also avoids controversy about what was ordered and serves as part of an audit trail for cost control purposes.

Taking a physical inventory periodically is critical to any food control system—it is the basis for calculating your "cost of food consumed" and your "food cost percentage." Unfortunately many small restaurants do not take inventories regularly because it can be time consuming. It need not be a painful process, however, if a good inventory sheet is designed (see Figure 8.3, on page 104). A great deal

DATE _____	**PURCHASE ORDER**			No. 1185	
	The Branding Iron Steak House, Inc.				
	To: _____				
	_____				
	_____				
	PLEASE FURNISH THE FOLLOWING—ALL CARRIERS CHARGES PREPAID				
QUANTITY	UNIT	DESCRIPTION		UNIT PRICE	AMOUNT
APPROVED_____			PURCHASING AGENT		
INVOICE MUST ACCOMPANY MERCHANDISE					

Figure 8.2: A typical purchase order used by larger restaurants.

THE BRANDING IRON STEAK HOUSE, INC.
INVENTORY SHEET

DATE _____   TAKEN BY _____

NAME OF PRODUCT	UNIT SIZE	STORAGE LOCATION				TOTAL UNITS	UNIT COST	TOTAL VALUE
		STORE ROOM	WALK-IN REFRIG.	FREEZER	SERVING STATION			
MEAT								
SIRL. TOP BUTTS								
SIRLOIN STRIPS								
GROUND BEEF								
TENDERLOIN								
RIB EYE STEAKS								
CHUCK								
BRISKET								
PORK CHOPS								
HAM, CANNED								
POULTRY								
TURKEY BREAST								
CHIX, BROILERS								
FISH								
HALIBUT								
SALMON								
HADDOCK								
LOBSTERS CHIX								
SOLE FILLET								
SHRIMP								
PRODUCE								
CABBAGE, RED								
CARROTS								
LETTUCE, ICEBG								
TOMATOES								
BAKE POTATOS								
CELERY								

PAGE 1 OF ____ PGS.   GRAND TOTAL

Figure 8.3: A typical inventory sheet.

of time is saved if the inventory sheet flows in the same order as the food products are arranged on the storeroom shelves. It is also helpful if the number of locations where food is stored is kept to a minimum.

Receiving, Storing and Issuing

The person who receives incoming shipments of food and beverages should check all products to make sure that the proper items were delivered. Cases should be opened, counted and checked for spoilage, inferior quality, or damage before the delivery slip is signed by the receiving clerk. Products should always be counted while the delivery driver is present and recorded on a receiving clerk's report (see Figure 8.4, on page 106).

From time to time, a shipment may arrive without the appropriate delivery slip. In such an event, a Merchandise Received Without Bill form (Figure 8.5, on page 107), should be filled out and signed by the delivery truck driver and the receiver. This acknowledges the quantity and type of goods that were actually received and avoids the possibility of confusion at a later date.

If incorrect merchandise has to be returned, a Request for Credit Memo (Figure 8.6, on page 107) should be signed by the truck driver when you relinquish the goods. In the past, when delivery slips were written by hand, it was possible to scratch out a returned item and retotal the slip. Today, with computerized billing, it does no good to simply change a delivery slip; the data must be entered into the computer. The Request for Credit Memo is proof that an incorrect item was indeed returned for credit and serves as a source document for a credit entry to be put into the computer. It also serves as a reminder to the buyer's accounting department to make sure the credit comes through at the end of the month.

Incoming shipments should be put away immediately after the products are received. Raw meats should be put into refrigerated storage of about 32°F to 34°F, and perishable vegetables should be put into refrigerated storage of about 40°F. Frozen foods should be quickly placed into a 0°F freezer. Nonperishable canned, jarred and packaged products (known as *dry stores*) should be placed into a dry storeroom and logged into an inventory book or on stock record cards (see Figure 8.7, on page 108).

The Branding Iron Steak House, Inc.

RECEIVING CLERK'S REPORT

No. 143

Purveyor _____

Receiver _____

DATE 199–	QUAN-TITY	UNIT SIZE	ITEM	√	UNIT PRICE	AMOUNT	TOTAL AMOUNT	STORAGE LOCATION		
								DRY STOREROOM FOOD & SUPPLIES	LIQUOR ROOM WINES, SPIRITS & BEER	SUNDRIES

Figure 8.4: A receiver's sheet used for recording incoming deliveries.

```
                                                    B 11860

              The Branding Iron Steak House, Inc.
              MERCHANDISE RECEIVED WITHOUT BILL
                Please send us a bill for the following Items

  From: _____      Date: _____
        _____

  Quantity                Item                    Amount
  |         |                           |              |    |
  |         |                           |              |    |
  |         |                           |              |    |
  |                          | Total    |              |    |
  Deliver                    |          |
  Driver  _____  | By: _____
```

Figure 8.5: This form should be used when merchandise is received without a bill.

```
                                                    B 11860

              The Branding Iron Steak House, Inc.
                    REQUEST FOR CREDIT MEMO
                Please send us a credit memo for the following

  To: _____      Date: _____
      _____

  Quanity                 Item                    Amount
  |         |                           |              |    |
  |         |                           |              |    |
  |         |                           |              |    |
  Reason for Return:         | Total Credit |           |    |
                             | By: _____
```

Figure 8.6: Credit memos stipulate the reason for a return of merchandise and serve as a followup reminder to check on credits.

A storeroom should have a moderate temperature, be well lighted, ventilated, dry and have a secure door lock. Small restaurants usually operate with an open storeroom, but large ones commonly have a controlled storeroom and a stock clerk.

Liquor storerooms should always be locked. The issuance of liquor storeroom keys is a matter of company policy, but the fewer the keys, the less risk there is of misuse. Usually, liquor storeroom keys are issued to only one or two people who have a need to access it regularly.

Storeroom shelving should be varied and spaced well enough to accommodate all items to be stocked. Modular shelving allows the flexibility to change shelf spacing as needed with relative ease. The uppermost shelves should be easily reachable. Every product carried should have a specific storage location on the shelves which matches location on the inventory sheet. This reduces the time required to take inventory significantly.

A record should be kept of all products removed from the storeroom. This may be done with a Requisition (Figure 8.8) which is filled out by the ordering department and turned in to the storeroom

The Branding Iron Steak House, Inc.											
STOCK RECORD CARD											
ITEM _____											
PURVEYOR _____							UNIT COST _____				
MAX _____ ARTICLE _____					SIZE _____						
MIN _____ LOCATION _____					UNIT _____		COST PER OZ. _____				

DATE	IN	OUT	BAL	DATE	IN	OUT	BAL	DATE	IN	OUT	BAL

Figure 8.7: Cards are hung on bins or shelves. They indicate additions and withdrawals to stock, as well as the current balance.

whenever something is needed. This procedure helps to control both the food storeroom and the liquor storeroom. In the case of alcoholic beverages, it also helps to keep the par stock at the bar at the desired level. The term *par stock* refers to the total number of bottles (full, in action or empties) that should always be present at the bar. The par stock is usually set at the number of bottles required to carry the bar through an entire day's business, without having to restock. A *bottle for bottle exchange* system, whereby empty bottles are replaced with full ones of the same brand and size, should be practiced in conjunction with the use of requisition slips.

The Branding Iron Steak House, Inc.

Date _____

REQUISITION

_____ DEPARTMENT

Please deliver to bearer

Quantity	Item	Cost

No. 1234

Signed_____

Department_____

Figure 8.8: Requisitions provide a record of items that are issued out of the storeroom.

Using Standardized Recipes

As discussed earlier in this book, customers want consistency every time they order an item. Variations in taste, portion size and plate presentation are not infrequent occurrences in many restaurants. These kinds of inconsistencies can be annoying to customers and can also be costly to a restaurant.

Such problems may be avoided, however, by developing standardized recipes for all items served on your menu, and making sure all employees adhere to them. A *standardized recipe* is one that specifies the ingredients to be used, the step-by-step method by which a product will be produced, the portion size and the way it will be presented on the plate. The main advantages of using standardized recipes are:

1. They assure high-quality products all day, every day.
2. They are helpful when training new employees.
3. They reduce overproduction and waste.
4. They allow for more accurate accounting of costs and sales.

Food Production Planning

Overproduction is wasteful, costly and results in excessive leftovers. For those reasons, it is important to plan the quantities of food to be produced each day. A common production planning system such as the following, involves only three things:

1. Maintaining a sales history
2. Forecasting the quantities of each item to be produced
3. Comparing the forecasted amounts with the actual results of the day

A *sales history* is a count of how many of each item on the menu were sold on a given day. The count is related to the total number of customers that were served that day. A popularity index is then calculated based on the average number sold over the last 60 days, as shown in Figure 8.9 (on page 111). A history should be kept for all items on the menu—appetizers, salads, entrees and desserts. After the forecasted day has transpired, the actual results of that day should be posted to the sales history chart, as was done for Wednesday, April 20 in the sample history. In this manner the history is kept up to date.

Sales History				
Entrees	60 Day Avg.		Wed.,April 20	
	No. Sold	Popularity Index	No. Sold	Percent of Total
Porterhouse Steak	38	20%	36	19%
Baked Stuffed Haddock	58	30%	55	30%
Boneless Breast of Chicken	67	35%	68	37%
Boiled Maine Lobster	28	15%	25	14%
Total	191	100%	184	100%

Figure 8.9: The sales history tracks the percentage of the total number of customers that ordered each item on the menu.

A sales forecast can be calculated by multiplying the number of customers estimated for the day being planned by the popularity index obtained from the sales history. This is done for each item on the menu, as shown in Figure 8.10 below. In this example, 205 customers are estimated on April 20th.

Sales Forecast: April 20, 199-			
	No. of Customers Expected	Popularity Index	No. of Items Forecast
Porterhouse Steak	205	20%	41
Baked Stuffed Haddock	205	30%	62
Boneless Breast of Chicken	205	35%	72
Lobster	205	15%	30
		Total	205

Figure 8.10: The sales forecast projects how many people are expected to order each item, based on the percentage of total guests that have ordered that item in the past.

The popularity index should be based on a meaningful period of time—60 days is often used. A single week's figures would not be adequate since they can be distorted by bad weather or competing events that may not recur on the day you are projecting.

Since it would be meaningless to compare normally busy days with normally quiet days, a separate sales history should be kept for each day of the week—Tuesdays should be compared with Tuesdays and Saturdays with Saturdays.

The last step in the process is to update the 60-day average popularity index by dropping the oldest day and adding the latest one to the index.

Supervision Is Important

It is easy to relax and not look for problems when things appear to be going well. For that reason, some restaurant owners lose sizable sums of money each year, without realizing it is happening. This type of operator may never know just how profitable the business might have been if better controls had been maintained. Profit leaks can occur from mistakes, waste and dishonest practices. To plug the leaks, control procedures should be installed in all profit centers and close supervision should be initiated to insure that the procedures are being carried out.

Following is a list of 28 situations that can cause a restaurant to lose profits. They are correctable, but not until management realizes they exist.

1. Not obtaining competitive prices before placing orders with vendors

2. Excessive buying—carrying too much stock in relation to sales volume ties up working capital that could be used for alternative investment opportunities

3. Not securing the storerooms and taking precaution to prevent theft

4. Not following up on credits for merchandise that was returned because of damage or that was backordered

5. Not taking advantage of discounts for payment on time—the result is the same as overpaying for products

6. Not checking invoices and payments against receiving records to detect any shortages, back-orders and incorrect prices

7. Not safeguarding the keys to the storeroom by issuing them to only one or two responsible persons whose duties require them to have access to the storeroom

8. Not using standard portion tools, such as ladles, scoops, measuring cups and spoons to assure proper portion sizes

9. Letting leftover foods spoil by not covering and refrigerating them quickly

10. Not keeping a daily record of food items sold, to compare with the quantity of food consumed that day

11. Overstaffing by scheduling extra kitchen staff and wait people when not needed

12 Not keeping adequate sales records to track customer menu preference trends

13. Making menus so complicated as to be confusing to customers and dampen sales

14. Not buying products in consistent sizes and consequently applying incorrect values when taking inventory

15. Failing to accurately record additions to and subtractions from inventory in a perpetual inventory book or on bin cards

16. Allowing excessive spoilage due to mishandling products and not having a management person verify spoilage when it occurs

17. Not taking a complete physical inventory at frequent intervals to calculate the food and beverage cost percentages and also to verify the accuracy of the perpetual inventory figures

18. Failing to take corrective action quickly when the cause of a problem is discovered

19. Failing to properly orient and train new employees

20. Not assigning clear responsibility for control of inventories to any one management person

21. Not using a system of forced issues to get rid of very slow moving items when cash flow needs improvement

22. Cooks not adhering to standard recipes

23. Improperly pricing menu items and thus not yielding the desired food cost percentage

24. Not organizing staff and thus not capitalizing on rush hour potential

25. Allowing unauthorized removal of products from premises by employees and delivery people who enter the establishment unsupervised

26. Failing to advertise specials effectively

27. Failing to meet customers' wants and needs, in regard to the menu items offered and the atmosphere of the establishment

28. Not establishing standard house policies by management or explaining them to all personnel.

Observers of the retail industry indicate pilferage is a major problem and acknowledge that employees represent a significant segment of the pilferers. Unfortunately, the restaurant industry is no exception to this indictment.

Products or services can be given away, they can be overcharged or undercharged for or they can be charged for but not recorded. The list of possibilities is lengthy. How then can management deal with the problem? The answer is to hire the best employees possible, train them well, maintain tight controls, and above all, supervise closely.

The object of a good security program is to keep people honest. This can be done by removing temptations, setting policies and standards for conduct and letting people know their actions are being observed. These are important deterrents to dishonest practices, but the first line of defense is to interview applicants thoroughly, check their references carefully and hire only the best people available. Be wary of applicants who:

1. are impatient at answering questions.

2. are impolite or take liberties in your office (such as smoking without permission or fondling objects on your desk). These traits reflect a lack of respect.

3. are untidy, or who appear to have a dependency that could affect their job performance.

4. are unprofessional or overfriendly during an interview.

Beware of the applicant who brags about all the famous places he or she has worked at. An unusually long list of previous employers may indicate the applicant could not hold a job for very long.

Entertainment

Restaurants will sometimes put entertainment in their lounge as a business builder. Good entertainment can attract new customers and keep your existing customers from drifting to competitors, but not all entertainment is good. To the contrary, ineffective entertainment can drive customers away and be a financial drain on your business. When considering adding entertainment, you should ask yourself the following questions:

1. What type of entertainment best fits my restaurant's format?

2. Do I have excess seating capacity? Can I accommodate additional volume with my present facilities?

3. Are my competitors using entertainment successfully? If so, what kind?

4. Are my customers asking for a certain type of entertainment, or, in the case of a new restaurant, will my target market expect it?

Three types of entertainment may be considered for a restaurant lounge: individual performers, bands and mechanical background music. Mechanical background music includes juke boxes and tape systems. It is the least expensive type and, when supplied by a juke box, can be an income producer. Individual performers, such as piano and guitar players, are the next least expensive. If they are good, they can add a uniquely pleasant quality to a lounge. Bands can be good attractions if they are popular, but the more popular they are, the more expensive they are.

Entertainment should be evaluated regularly. Ask the following questions:

1. Is it increasing sales?
2. Is it attracting the type of clientele I am seeking?
3. Are profits increasing as a result of the addition of entertainment?

How To Calculate Your Breakeven Point for Entertainment

Assume your restaurant lounge has excess capacity. That is, on certain nights of the week you have many empty seats. This concerns you because your overhead costs go on whether you have a half-filled house or a jam-packed house. Consequently, you could increase your business volume without incurring any additional overhead costs.

Let us assume you decide to offer entertainment to attract more people to your lounge on those slow nights, so you hire a piano player. In addition, you run an advertisement in the local newspaper to let the community know you have entertainment.

Your main concern at this point is that the entertainment, at the very least, must pay its own way—breakeven. If it does not do that, it will not have accomplished its intended purpose of increasing business and is, in fact, a further drain on your profits that must be changed or terminated.

The following example illustrates how you can calculate a breakeven point for the entertainment. It is assumed that you operate with a 23 percent pouring cost (that is, 23 percent out of each dollar of sales goes to pay for the liquor required to make the drinks).

Step 1: Determine the total cost of the entertainment.

Cost of piano player ($200 a night for 3 nights)	*$600*
Cost of advertisement	*200*
Total Cost Related to the Entertainment	*$800*

Step 2: Establish your contribution margin.

100% − Pouring Cost Percentage = Contribution Margin
or: 100% − 23% = 77%

> **Step 3:** Calculate your breakeven point.
> *Total Cost ÷ Contribution Margin = Breakeven Point*
> $$\$800 \div .77 = \$1,039$$
> $$\$1,039 = Breakeven\ Point$$

If sales increase by $1,039, the lounge will have taken in just enough additional money to break even. The increase will cover the cost of the liquor in the additional drinks sold, the cost of the advertisement and the piano player. There would be neither a profit nor a loss at this point. Hopefully, as the entertainment catches on, sales will increase substantially above the breakeven point.

Equipment Maintenance

An effective maintenance program will more than pay for itself. It can help avoid accidents, reduce downtime and add dollars to your profit line.

It makes sense to keep your equipment in top shape. Reducing equipment repairs is another key to making greater profits. Aside from the fact that repair calls are expensive, it is hard to find good service people. Five steps for developing a sound equipment mainte nance program are shown below:

1. *Announce It:* Explain to all employees the need for the program and the benefits it will bring. Unless everyone cooperates, the program will not work well.

2. *Set Up Records:* Develop a file folder for every piece of major equipment. Each folder should contain the name of the product, the manufacturer's name, the model year, the style of each piece of equipment, the warrantee form, the service agency's name, a record of service calls with costs and dates, the specification sheets and owner's operating manual.

3. *Follow a Checklist:* Formalize the program by developing a check list for inspections. With such a list, no piece of equipment is overlooked and the right things are looked at on each piece of equipment.

4. *List the Procedures:* Develop a set of maintenance procedures for each piece of equipment. They should be easy to understand and accessible. It is a good idea to keep three sets of the procedures (you can be sure one will get lost).

5. *Assign Responsibility:* Assign the responsibility for the inspection of equipment to a specific person. The frequency and extent of inspections should be clearly understood.

A good maintenance program lets employees know that the restaurant cares, and, as a result, the employees will strive to assure its success. Management must, of course, set the tone by keeping the program updated and by providing the necessary tools and supplies to properly maintain the equipment.

Action Guidelines

✔ Obtain food and beverage lists from dealers and select initial inventories.

✔ Create an inventory sheet that includes all of your food and beverage stock for taking physical inventories.

✔ Develop a perpetual inventory book (using a three-ring binder) with a separate stock record card dedicated to each item carried in stock.

✔ Demonstrate your understanding of turnover rates by calculating the food turnover rate for a restaurant with the figures shown below:

Beginning Inventory 11/1	$3,200.00
Purchases 11/1–11/30	8,800.00
Ending Inventory 11/30	3,450.00

✔ Develop a sales history sheet to track the popularity of items on your menu.

✔ Forecast your production needs for next week by using the popularity indexes developed with your sales history sheet.

MANAGING YOUR PERSONNEL

Everyone wins when a restaurant trains its employees well, gives them the right tools to work with, and pays them adequately. The restaurant flourishes, its employees earn more money and have a sense of pride and its customers are pleased.

Although waitpeople are the only employees that have actual contact with customers, every employee of a restaurant must envision him or herself as serving the customer. They must understand clearly how their job, no matter what level it is, fits into the process of satisfying customers and is, therefore, important to the success of the restaurant. This is a basic principle of total quality management.

The way a waitperson approaches a customer, presents menu information, answers questions and makes the customer feel welcome has a great influence on how often that customer will return.

Equally important is the work of employees in the back of the house that the customer does not see. An inferior meal, soiled utensils or an unclean restroom may irritate a customer to the point that they will not return. Usually, disgruntled customers will try another restaurant and if they have a pleasant experience there, you may never see them again.

Keep Customers Coming Back

The true cost of a lost customer is often minimized by statements like "you can't win them all," but a lost customer does in fact represent a potential loss of significant revenue. For example, if a restaurant loses a regular customer that brings a guest once a week and spends an average of $40 each visit, the establishment has a potential revenue loss of approximately $20,800 over a ten-year period. Unfortunately most restaurateurs have no idea how many customers they have lost, because people rarely complain to management—they just disappear.

How To Get the Most Out of Your Personnel

Management should develop clear and reasonable policies and explain them to all employees so that everyone knows exactly what is expected of them. Getting the most out of employees begins with hiring the best people you can afford and

1. training them properly,
2. providing them with the right equipment and facilities to do their job well,
3. letting them know that you are aware of what happens and care about how things are done,
4. soliciting ideas for improvement from them and letting them know that they are important to the organization and
5. supervising them carefully.

High Labor Turnover—A Clue to Problems

The rate at which employees terminate employment is a clue to problem areas that need attention. Labor turnover has an impact on the profitability of a restaurant because the cost of replacing employees is very high. The real cost is not often realized by employers—it includes the following:

1. The cost of the exit interview time
2. Possibly, an unemployment compensation tax increase
3. The cost of advertising the job openings

4. The hidden cost of lost production due to the lowering of morale among the remaining employees who have to pick up the slack

5. The cost of interviewing time

6. The cost of training new employees

7. The cost of additional waste while the new employees learn their jobs

To calculate a labor turnover rate, divide the number of employees that terminated employment during a given period of time by the number of jobs in the restaurant and multiply the result by 100.

$$\frac{\text{No. of employees that terminated}}{\text{No. of Jobs}} \times 100 = \text{Labor Turnover Rate}$$

For example, if a restaurant had 9 of its 34 employees terminate employment last year, its labor turnover rate would be 26.5%.

$$\frac{9}{34} \times 100 = 26.5\%$$

Payroll Analysis

Restaurants are very vulnerable to seasonal ups and downs—consequently, employers must react quickly to changes in sales. Overstaffing and low productivity are major threats to profitability. It is important to measure productivity at regular intervals because it can get out of line very quickly.

Employee productivity can be measured as it relates to (1) the number of customers served (covers) per employee, (2) sales dollars generated per employee and (3) sales per hour worked (see Figure 9.1). Following is an illustration of how these measures of productivity are calculated:

Covers per Employee   = Covers Served ÷ No. of Employees
Sales per Employee   = Sales ÷ No. of Employees
Sales per Hour Worked = Sales ÷ Actual Hours Worked

Payroll Analysis

DATE Week of	SALES	Covers Served	Number of Employees	Actual Hours Worked	Payroll	Covers per Employee	Sales per Employee	Sales per Man-Hour
Jun 9	19,500	2344	18	730	$2550	130	$1083	$26.71
Jun 16	17,640	2110	19	750	2458	111	928	23.52
Jun 23	15,580	2045	20	790	2556	102	779	19.72
Jun 30	14,850	2084	21	805	2610	99	707	18.44
Jul 7	21,950	2550	21	848	2706	121	1045	25.88

Figure 9.1: Illustration of the process for analyzing weekly payroll.

Initial Interviews

It pays for a restaurant to hire the best people it can afford. All applicants should be carefully interviewed in order to avoid hiring people with undesirable traits. Interviewers should be wary of individuals that display impatience at answering questions or who avoid giving specific answers to questions.

Applicants that have an untidy appearance, are noticeably impolite or who become overfriendly warrant further scrutiny. Also, beware of people that have unexplained gaps in the chronology of their work experience, and be sure to check references.

Exit Interviews

If there are reasons for an employee's departure that might have been avoided or that signal necessary changes, they will often be revealed in an exit interview. Sometimes an employee will leave a job because it is boring. Knowing this, management may be able to restructure the job to make it more interesting for the next person.

On occasion employees will leave a job because they see another employee doing something that they disapprove of and do not want to become involved in. Exit interviews can sometimes reveal information that would otherwise be difficult to obtain.

Orientation for New Employees

New employees should be informed immediately of what you will expect of them and what they may expect of you. Orientation sessions should be well planned if you wish to convey the same information to all employees in a clear and consistent way. The content of the sessions will vary with the type and size of an organization, but certain kinds of information are of interest to all employees. Following is a checklist of typical topics that might be covered in an orientation:

1. History of the establishment
2. Who the owner is
3. Who the management personnel are and who the employee reports to and takes orders from

4. Hours—regular work week, when and where posted
5. Vacation policy—how much time and when
6. Fringe benefits—insurances, sick days, etc.
7. Meals, if applicable—when and what items
8. Compensation—hourly rate, deductions, when is payday
9. Absenteeism and tardiness policy
10. Probationary period and warning policies
11. Smoking and coffee break policies
12. How training will occur—when, where, by whom, how long
13. Employee evaluation and advancement policies
14. Overtime policy—if allowed, who authorizes it
15. Tip reporting policy
16. Lost guest check policy
17. How to handle customer complaints
18. Breakage policy
19. Dress code—who will supply uniforms and how many
20. Who will launder uniforms
21. Deposits, if required for uniforms
22. Appearance of employee—fingernails and cleanliness
23. Policy on jewelry, hairnets and types of shoes
24. Tour of establishment, including:
    a) where things are
    b) where to park
    c) which restrooms to use and where they are
    d) where to enter and leave the establishment
    e) where lockers are (if any)
25. Actions that may result in termination of employment
26. How to call in, in case of emergency—when and who to call (with phone numbers)
27. Personal behavior—profanity, vulgar actions
28. Personal phone call policy
29. Policy on patronizing the establishment before or after work hours

30. What to do in case of accidents or fire
31. Use of safety guards on equipment
32. Portion control policy
33. Holiday work policy

Some items need only be touched upon, while others may need to be discussed in detail. In any case, you should clearly explain the policies that apply and give employees an opportunity to ask questions—this may avert problems at a later date.

Training Your Employees

An often made mistake is to turn a new employee over to a present employee for training. The problem with that practice is bad habits can be passed on by the present employee to the new person. It is said that less than 80 percent of an employee's knowledge tends to get passed on in such training situations. Consequently, if an establishment has a high labor turnover rate, jobs can change drastically over a period of time.

This dilemma may be alleviated to a great degree by giving present workers instructions on how to train others. A four-step method of training that has been used very effectively by manufacturing industries can be utilized by the foodservice field. The four steps are the following:

1. Show the employee how to do the task. Demonstrate it.
2. Simultaneously, tell the employee what you are doing and why you are doing it.
3. Let the employee do it once or twice, under supervision. If the employee does it right, allow him or her to continue on his or her own.
4. Check back periodically to make sure the employee continues to do the task properly.

This technique is effective with tasks such as cash register training, where there are numerous small but easy-to-forget steps involved. Most restaurants try to hire employees with training and experience. But, even with such a background, it is important to familiarize them with your policies and procedures.

Management has a responsibility to provide the necessary equipment to do a job properly. It is unacceptable for employees to be producing inferior products simply because they lack the proper tools. Another impediment to doing good work is a poorly laid out work center. The physical arrangement of a restaurant kitchen should allow safe and efficient movement for workers. It should also be well lighted and ventillated. Any of these features, if not properly planned, can adversely affect productivity and profits.

How To Gain Your Employees' Cooperation

Cooperative and loyal employees are the most important assets a business can have. Regrettably, many restaurants do not have such employees—largely because they do not realize that cooperation must be won, not dictated. Following are six ways to win cooperation from your employees.

1. Make your employees *want* to cooperate with you. The old notion of demanding cooperation does not work. Instead, try the following:

    • Let them know what your policies and objectives are.

    • Let them know how they can personally benefit by working toward the accomplishment of your objectives.

    • Appeal to their professional pride and desire to be on a winning team.

2. Set a fair challenge—do not expect unreasonable results and, above all, be realistic in your expectations.

3. Have an open mind and be receptive to employees' suggestions and views. This shows you are concerned and sympathetic even when you have to say "No."

4. Acknowledge a job well done, particularly on an undesirable task—it is a good way of winning an employee's cooperation the next time you need to get a tough job done. If it is honest praise, it is important that you give it because the employee knows he or she deserves it.

5. Avoid arguments with employees. Time has a calming effect—use it. Let the employee tell his or her side of the story and acknowledge that you heard it and understand what they said. Then arrange a time to discuss it. Just a few minutes is often

enough time for tempers to settle. Even the thorniest problems can be dealt with more easily when the parties involved are in control of their emotions.

6. Do not hesitate to admit an error on your part. It will not change your status, or authority. Instead, it will humanize you in the eyes of your staff.

Ways To Improve Employee Morale

Low morale will inevitably result in poor work habits, excessive waste, accidents and consequently a loss of profits. An effective manager will keep close watch on the morale of his or her organization and take corrective action quickly if it declines. Some ways to improve morale are listed below:

1. Try to find out what every employee's strength or special skill is and when possible give him or her the opportunity to make use of it.

2. Be responsive to employees' concerns. You may not agree with them but do not try to avoid them. If the complaints are valid, they won't go away. In any case, explain the reasons for your thinking.

3. Provide employees with the environment to do a good job. This not only includes the proper tools but also sanitary and safe equipment, lighting, sound control and physical comforts (such as rubber floor mats on a hard tile floor).

4. Do not ignore false rumors.

5. As soon as possible, discuss the impact of any proposed changes with the employees that will be affected by them.

6. Let your employees know how they are doing. Employees often believe they are overlooked when they do something good but are immediately reprimanded when they make a mistake. Try to eradicate that notion by giving them suggestions on how to correct any deficiencies they may have.

7. Be firm but fair—make reasonable assignments and enforce rules in an impartial manner.

8. Work through your chain-of-command—don't undercut your

supervisors by throwing your weight around or by dealing directly with subordinate employees.

9. Be aware of seven statements that, when uttered with sincerity in appropriate situations, can help to improve morale immensely.

- "Please."
- "Thank you."
- "Can I help?"
- "You did a fine job."
- "What do you folks think?"
- "I'm sorry. I made a mistake."
- "I realize it was not your fault."

Keep the Lines of Communication Open

Allow your employees to communicate with you. It is a good practice to hold employee meetings where they have a chance to offer constructive ideas. Discuss problems such as high food cost percentages, adverse customer comments and critical health inspector's reports. These kinds of issues can be solved better in an atmosphere of cooperation, where employees are allowed input.

Keep the meetings brief and businesslike—have a written agenda ready and be organized but not intimidating. Think of the meetings as a two-way street with information flowing from you to them and from them to you.

Beware of Hidden Agendas

Employees will frequently hide the real reasons for their behavior or poor performance. Fears, jealousies, antagonisms and misunderstandings among employees are often reflected in flashes of anger or mood swings that result in poor job performance. Such behavior may also be visible (and objectionable) to customers; consequently, it cannot be allowed to continue.

When such a situation occurs, bring both parties together, confront the issue and let them know how it is affecting their work. Seek agreement from both parties on the resolution of the problem. Here are some strategies for dealing with such situations:

1. Appear impartial as you listen patiently to both sides of the story before judging.

2. Be tactful as you explain the reasons for your decision.

3. Try to end the discussion on a positive note, leaving no doubt that the situation must improve.

How To Use Job Descriptions

Job descriptions may by used for several purposes—among them to express the duties of a job for which a person is being hired and to tell how management wants those duties performed. Although job descriptions may exist for all jobs, it is rare for them to be shown to hourly employees when they are hired. This is unfortunate because every new employee can benefit from knowing what is expected of him or her.

Job descriptions can also serve as checklists when training new employees. For a sample job description, with a composite list of typical duties and responsibilities, see Figure 9.2, Job Description for a Chef. As with all jobs, the duties of a chef will vary depending on the size and type of restaurant, and the degree of autonomy the owner grants to the chef.

Figure 9.2:

Job Description for a Chef

Summary

Responsible to the owner. Oversees the day-to-day operations of the back of the house. Responsible for carrying out company policies and performing the following duties: menu planning, purchasing, hiring and training new employees, supervising and motivating staff, filling in as needed for cooks, performing cost control functions and maintaining a high level of quality and service in all aspects of the operation.

Responsibilities

1) Performs all assigned duties and responsibilities according to company policies and reports to the owner in a timely and efficient manner.

Figure 9.2, *continued*.

2) Develops menus.

3) Prices all menu items.

4) Establishes portion sizes.

5) Obtains competitive prices for items to be bought from purveyors.

6) Purchases products necessary to satisfy menu requirements and customers' expectations.

7) Responsible for cost control programs in the areas of payroll, food, beverages, supplies and utilities, so that maximum quality is obtained at minimum cost.

8) Coordinates service for functions.

9) Supervises and motivates employees.

10) Inspects kitchen operations regularly for cleanliness and proper functioning of equipment.

11) Monitors all production stations during rush periods to ensure that production is flowing properly.

12) Assists, as needed, in all capacities and handles customers' complaints.

13) Schedules kitchen employees so as to ensure high quality service, while containing payroll cost within an established percentage range.

14) Responsible for hiring and terminating employees, processing time cards, conducting evaluations and holding kitchen staff meetings, as necessary.

15) Responsible for safety and security systems in the back of the house.

16) Responsible for compliance with sanitation codes in all areas.

17) Responsible for taking inventories and calculating food cost percentages.

Action Guidelines

✔ Prepare job descriptions for the following jobs:

Cook	Baker
Salad Maker	General Kitchen Worker
Dishwasher	

✔ Design an appropriate form to be used for weekly payroll analysis.

✔ Develop a personnel manual to be given to new employees.

✔ Outline a checklist of questions to be used as an interview guide.

✔ Construct an employment application.

MAINTAINING FINANCIAL CONTROL

It is not necessary to be an accountant to operate a restaurant successfully, but a manager must be familiar with the financial statements—in particular with the income statement and the balance sheet. The income statement (sometimes called the profit or loss statement) is important because it indicates whether the business made a profit or suffered a loss in a given period of time. The balance sheet tells the reader what the business owns and what it owes to others, as well as how much equity or net worth the owner has in the business.

The balance sheet can be compared to a candid snapshot—it is a picture of a business that shows how it appeared at one instant of time, usually the end of a month or the end of a year. The income statement, by comparison, can be likened to a movie film. It has a beginning and an ending (the profit or a loss), and tells the reader what happened in between that lead to the ending.

Understanding the Income Statement

An income statement contains four types of information—*revenues, costs, expenses,* and *profit or loss.* In essence it tells the reader how much money came in and from what sources, the cost of the raw materials that went into the products that were sold, the expenses that were incurred in the course of operating the business and whether a profit or loss resulted. Following is an example of the essential elements of an income statement:

Total Revenues	$806,071
Less: Cost of Sales	239,089
Less: Expenses	478,981
Net Profit Before Tax	$ 88,001

While the above information tells us the business produced a profit, it is relatively useless as a management tool that can be used to solve problems and establish goals. Only when an income statement is fleshed out, as illustrated below, in Figure 10.1, can it be used as an analytical tool.

Figure 10.1:

Income Statement

for the period of January 1 through December 31, 199–

Sales		Pct.
Food Sales	$ 602,745	75.0%
Beverage Sales	200,915	25.0
Total Sales	**$803,660**	**100.0**
Cost of Sales		
Food Cost	**$192,878**	**32.0**
Beverage Cost	46,210	23.0
Total Cost of Sales	**$239,088**	**29.7**
Gross Profit from Operations	**$564,572**	**70.3**
Other Income	2,411	0.3
Total Gross Profit	**$566,983**	**70.6**
Controllable Expenses		
Payroll	$212,166	26.4
Employee Benefits	32,146	4.0
Direct Operating Expenses	45,809	5.7
Advertising and Promotion	23,306	2.9
Music and Entertainment	16,073	2.0
Utilities	25,717	3.2
Administrative and General Expenses	32,146	4.0
Repairs and Maintenance	16,073	2.0
Total Controllable Expenses	**$403,436**	**50.2**
Profit Before Occupancy Costs	$163,547	20.4

Figure 10.1, *continued.*

Occupancy Costs (Triple Net Lease)

Rent	$ 40,987	5.1
Property Taxes	4,822	0.6
Other Taxes	1,607	0.2
Property Insurance	8,037	1.0
Total Occupancy Costs	**$ 55,453**	**6.9**
Profit Before Interest		
and Depreciation	$108,094	13.5
Interest	4,018	0.5
Depreciation	16,075	2.0
Net Profit	**$ 88,001**	**11.0**

Comparisons Are Informative

An income statement with percentages allows you to compare costs, expenses and profits against sales. If sales rise profits should also rise, but if costs or expenses are out of line, profits may not increase as expected. The income statement is a valuable analytical tool—its percentages will reveal good performance, as well as problem areas that need attention. Industry statistics for similar operations may be obtained from the National Restaurant Association and can be used to make comparisons with your restaurant.

Your current income statement can also be compared with those of previous months, or years, to assess the growth, stagnation or decline of your business. Such analyses can also raise a number of questions about a business:

- Have costs gotten out of line, possibly reflecting poor purchasing practices?
- Is the nature of the business changing—is it selling more liquor than food?
- Are all profit centers contributing to profits as well as they should?
- Are any visible trends emerging?

Understanding Your Balance Sheet

The basic purpose of a balance sheet (see Figure 10.2) is to inform the reader as to what the business owns, what it owes others, and what its worth is. The things a business owns are called its *assets*, the things it owes to others are called its *liabilities*, and the owner's equity is referred to as its *net worth*. The statement is called a balance sheet because total assets must always equal total liabilities plus net worth. If they do not, the statement will be out of balance and therefore incorrect.

Figure 10.2:

Balance Sheet

for the year ending December 31, 199–

Assets

Current Assets

Cash on Hand		$5,000
Cash in Bank		23,000
Accounts Receivable		3,800
Food Inventory		9,500
Beverage Inventory		8,800
Supplies Inventory		2,600
Marketable Securities		21,000
Prepaid Expenses		13,800
Total Current Assets		**$ 87,500**
Fixed Assets		
Furniture, Fixtures		
& Equipment	$148,500	
Less: Depreciation Reserve	30,000	118,500
Leasehold Improvements	98,000	
Less: Depreciation Reserve	4,000	94,000
Total Fixed Assets		**$212,500**
Total Assets		**$300,000**

Liabilities and Net Worth

Current Liabilities

Accounts Payable		18,000
Taxes Collected		7,500
Accrued Expenses		12,645

Figure 10.2, *continued.*

Current Portion of Long-Term Loan Due	2,501
Total Current Liabilities	**40,646**
Long-Term Loan Balance (12%)	111,855
Less: Current Portion Due	2,501
Total Long-Term Loan	**109,354**
Net Worth	
Partner A	50,000
Partner B	50,000
Partner C	50,000
Total Partner's Equity	**150,000**
Total Liabilities and Net Worth	**$300,000**

Ratios—Valuable Analytical Tools

Numbers are more meaningful when they are related to other significant numbers, such as sales. When sales rise or fall, it is reasonable to expect certain expenses to increase or decrease accordingly. Other relationships between numbers on statements can reveal the health of a business—its strengths and weaknesses. To facilitate such comparisons, the following analytical tools have been developed:

1. Food Cost Percentage
2. Pouring Cost Percentage
3. Labor Cost Percentage
4. Expense Percentages
5. Net Profit on Sales
6. Rate of Return on Investment
7. Current Ratio
8. Acid Test Ratio
9. Working Capital
10. Average Guest Check
11. Seat Turnover Ratio

Food, beverage and labor cost percentages may be calculated daily, weekly or monthly. It is not advisable to go for more than a month without taking a physical inventory, because facts are forgotten and problems become increasingly harder to solve with the passage of time.

Food Cost Percentage. This percentage can be calculated for a single entree or for all the food consumed in a given period of time. It tells you what percentage of the selling price of a food product goes to pay for the ingredients from which it was made. Food cost percentages will vary depending on the style of service, sales promotional objectives, and efficiency of each restaurant, but most table service restaurants tend to operate between 30 percent and 35 percent overall, with some as low as 25 percent and others as high as 40 percent. The formula for calculating a food cost percentage is the following:

$$\text{Cost of Food Sold} \div \text{Food Sales} = \text{Food Cost Percentage}$$
$$\$192,878 \div \$602,745 = 32\%$$

Pouring Cost Percentage. The pouring cost percentage tells you what percentage of the selling price of a drink goes to pay for the liquor used to make it. Typically, pouring cost percentages range from 18 percent to 30 percent depending on style of service, sales promotion objectives, desired profit margin and efficiency. It can be calculated for one drink or for all of the liquor consumed during a certain period of time. The percentage is calculated as follows:

$$\text{Cost of Beverages Sold} \div \text{Beverage Sales} = \text{Pouring Cost Percentage}$$
$$\$46,210 \div \$200,915 = 23\%$$

Labor Cost Percentage. This percentage gives you an indication of how efficiently you are using your workforce. It tells you what percentage of your sales dollar goes to pay for labor costs. The causes for high labor cost percentages include allowing too much overtime, overstaffing, inadequate training and not supervising the workforce well enough. Industry statistics can be used to compare your expenses with those of other similar establishments. The formula for calculating your labor cost percentage is:

(Payroll + Employee Benefits) ÷ Total Sales = Labor Cost Percentage

($212,166 + $32,146) ÷ $803,660 = 30.4%

Expense Percentages. Every restaurant has a number of expense categories that can be abused if not controlled properly, such as heat, light, paper goods, linens. This percentage tells you how well those expenses are being contained within acceptable limits. The following formula may be used to calculate the percentage relationship of any expense item to total sales (here the example expense is advertising):

Expense ÷ Total Sales = Expense Percentage
$23,306 ÷ $803,660 = 2.9%

Percentage of Net Profit on Sales. This percentage reflects a business's ability to operate profitably. A restaurant may do a superb job on increasing sales, but unless it does a good job of controlling expenses, it may not produce a proportionate increase in profits. The formula shown below relates profits to sales (in the case of a corporation, net profit after taxes would be used).

Net Profit ÷ Total Sales = Percentage of Net Profit on Sales

$88,001 ÷ $803,660 = 11%

Rate of Return on Investment. This is a measure of how well a business is utilizing the funds its investors invested. It is also an essential piece of information to consider when buying or selling a business, because it indicates how fast the business will be able to pay back the funds invested. It is also useful when comparing alternative investment opportunities (in the case of a corporation, net profit after taxes would be used).

Net Profit ÷ Investment = Rate of Return on Investment
$88,001 ÷ $300,000 = 29.3%

Current Ratio. This ratio reflects a restaurant's ability to pay its bills as they come due and is, therefore, of great interest to suppliers and lenders. Only current assets may be used in this calculation—

those are cash, receivables, marketable securities, inventories and prepaid expenses (such as insurance premiums that are paid in advance). The ratio relates current assets to current liabilities—obligations that must be paid on a current basis. They include such things as accounts payable, notes payable, and accrued expenses (for example, wages payable). In the following example, the business has 2.2 times as many current assets as it has current liabilities. In general, a current ratio of at least 2 to 1 is considered adequate for the payment of current bills in a timely manner.

$$\text{Current Assets} \div \text{Current Liabilities} = \text{Current Ratio}$$
$$\$\ 87,500 \div \$40,646 = 2.2{:}1$$

The Acid Test Ratio. If a restaurant's current ratio is less than the desired 2 to 1, another test can be applied to determine a firm's ability to pay its current bills—that is the acid test ratio. Only cash and other quick assets that can be rapidly converted to cash can be used in this calculation. The other "quick assets" are accounts receivable and marketable securities. The sum of the three categories is divided by current liabilities as shown below:

$$\frac{\text{Cash} + \text{Accounts Receivable} + \text{Marketable Securities}}{\text{Current Liabilities}} = \text{Acid Test Ratio}$$
$$\frac{\$28,000 + \$3,800 + \$21,000}{\$40,646} = \frac{\$52,800}{\$40,646} = 1.3{:}1$$

The firm analyzed above has 1.3 times as many quick assets as it has current liabilities. Since 1 to 1 is considered to be an acceptable acid test ratio, this business is in sound financial condition and is capable of paying its current bills on time.

Working Capital. These are the funds that are needed to operate a business from week to week. Sometimes new businesses spend so much money on equipment and buildings that they run out of working capital when they fail to realize the cash flow they were expecting in their first year. It is said that lack of adequate working capital is one of the main causes of business failures.

Working capital is the difference between a business's current assets and its current liabilities, as shown below:

> Current Assets – Current Liabilities = Working Capital
> $ 87,500 – $40,646 = $46,854

Average Guest Check. This is the amount that, on average, a customer spends when they patronize your restaurant. Due to the differences between meal periods and bar business, it is more meaningful to do a separate calculation for each meal period and for the bar. Average guest check is an important number to monitor because a declining amount might indicate that a service or quality problem exists, or perhaps that the waitstaff is not practicing suggestive selling. The average guest check is calculated as follows:

> Total Sales ÷ No. of Guests Served = Average Guest Check
> Lunch $188,084 ÷ 30,680 = $ 6.13
> Dinner   531,180 ÷ 23,660 = $22.45
> Bar Only   84,396 ÷ 15,340 = $ 5.50

The Seat Turnover Ratio. This is an indicator of how effectively you are attracting people to your restaurant and how efficiently you are serving them when they are there. A declining ratio may indicate that your service is too slow or that you are experiencing an erosion of your customer base. The latter is a major concern and, if not corrected, will lead to business failure. The illustration below shows how a seat turnover ratio can be calculated for the preceding year. It could also be calculated for a week or a month, simply by substituting the appropriate figures.

> No. of Customers Annually ÷ No. of Seats ÷ 365 = Seat Turnover Ratio
> Dining Room   54,340 ÷ 100 ÷ 365 = 1.5 times a day
> Bar Only   15,340 ÷ 100 ÷ 365 = .42 times a day

How Much Control Is Enough?

A certain amount of control will be inherently present if the owner is actively involved in a business. But that type of control should not be relied upon because the owner cannot physically work every hour of every day—when he or she is absent there is a management void and that is when conditions often break down.

The ideal control system will incorporate management oversight with a variety of control procedures and reporting mechanisms that do not require the owner to always be present.

It should be noted, however, that the cost of any control procedure should not exceed the potential savings it can bring about. Put simply, one should not spend dollars to chase after pennies.

A Simple Control System for a Small Restaurant

The following cost control system is easy to install and can work well for small restaurants that want to avoid more paperwork. It is a substantial improvement over having no controls and requires only three things:

1. A periodic inventory
2. A record of purchases
3. A record of sales

The system involves taking an inventory at the beginning of a period, and again at the end of the period. The period may be whatever duration you desire from one week to a month but should not exceed a month. A record of sales and purchases is kept during the period, and, at the end of the period, the cost of food sold is calculated as illustrated below:

Beginning Inventory	8/1	$3,200
Plus: Purchases	8/1–8/31	9,800
Total		13,000
Less: Ending Inventory	8/31	3,400
Cost of Food Sold		$9,600

Use the cost of food sold in the following equation to determine the percentage:

$$\frac{\text{Cost of Food Sold}}{\text{Food Sales}} = \frac{\$9,600}{\$30,000} = 32\% \text{ Food Cost}$$

The food cost percentage is an indicator of a number of things—how well the purchasing function is being conducted, how much waste may be occurring in the kitchen as a result of carelessness and overportioning, as well as the possibility of pilferage. When a food cost percentage remains high for a period of time, it is advisable to analyze the menu to ascertain whether adequate prices are being charged.

Even the minimal amount of control such as that illustrated above can bring about important results in an operation that currently has no controls. The system can be installed easily, without professional assistance—all that is needed is a supply of inventory forms.

Supervision Reduces Undesirable Practices

No matter how well management tries to screen applicants and hire the best people, the possibility always exists that undesirable practices may set in. Management must monitor operations carefully to deter, or at least quickly discover, any unwanted activities. Here are some things to look for when percentages get out of line:

1. Unauthorized removal of property from the restaurant
2. Overportioning food or beverages due to carelessness or to get bigger tips
3. Giving unauthorized discounts or not charging friends
4. Covering up for merchandise taken undetected by changing inventory counts
5. Collusion among employees
6. Accepting gifts in return for buying inferior or overpriced products
7. Tampering with counters or meters on machines or bottles
8. Faking lost guest checks, petty cash payouts or breakage
9. Leaving the cash register drawer open and not ringing up every sale

With close supervision, control procedures will go a long way toward preventing unwanted practices from getting started. Observers of retail industries indicate pilferage by employees is a major problem. Management's challenge is to eliminate any temptations by having well-understood procedures for controlling all aspects of its operations, particularly inventories and cash.

Automated Systems for Restaurants

Many automated systems for controlling restaurant operations currently exist and the technology is advancing rapidly. Among them are integrated accounting systems, liquor dispensing systems and cashiering systems that can provide sophisticated inventory, production and sales reports. Most of the systems are very good at doing what they purport to do, but most are expensive and require a certain volume of business to justify their installation.

The degree to which a restaurant will automate will depend upon its size and volume, its available funds and its management's perception of its control problems and potential. Numerous reasons for installing automatic systems are put forth by their manufacturers. Prominent among them are the following:

1. Promote consistency of products

2. Control inventories

3. Prevent overportioning

4. Eliminate pricing errors

5. Insure that house policies will be followed

6. Remove temptation

7. Reveal missing guest checks and cash shortages

Users of automated systems regard them highly. But, as good as they are, they are not without their critics. The main criticisms are that they are costly and are perceived as impersonal by some customers. The potential savings and benefits to be realized should be examined carefully before investing in any system.

Action Guidelines

✔ Prepare an estimated income statement and calculate the following measurements of the health of the business:

1. Food cost percentage
2. Pouring cost percentage
3. Labor cost percentage
4. Net profit on sales

✔ Prepare an estimated balance sheet and calculate the following measurements of the financial strength of the business:

1. Working capital
2. Current ratio
3. Acid test ratio

RESTAURANT MARKETING

In the restaurant business, marketing may be defined as "the process of getting the right products and services to the right customers, at the right time and place, and at the right price." The key word in each instance is "right."

Is a Marketing Plan Necessary?

A restaurant without a marketing plan is like a ship without a rudder—it will drift aimlessly. A marketing plan will help it stay on the right course to achieve its goals. When clearly communicated to employees, a marketing plan can create a team spirit that brings out the best performance from everyone and focuses their efforts on the achievement of the restaurant's goals.

A Seven-Step Process for Developing a Marketing Plan

1. Establish your overall objective.
   Example: *To increase sales by 30 percent next year.*
2. Identify your strengths and weaknesses.

   <u>Strengths</u>   <u>Weakness</u>
   Excellent food and drinks   *Lack of seating capacity*
   Excellent service

3. List the alternative strategies available to you.

   a. *Add on to existing building.*

   b. *Convert function rooms to general dining.*

   c. *Increase seat turnover.*

4. Select the best strategy.

   Assume "increase seat turnover" is the best.

5. Develop a detailed plan of action.

   a. *Review menu offerings that require lengthy preparation times. Try to pre-prep more items, to speed up the production process. Where necessary, replace difficult to prepare items with popular, but easier to prepare items.*

   b. *Offer early-bird specials to attract people before the usual rush hours and thereby gain an additional turnover.*

   c. *Retrain waitstaff to deliver orders to kitchen and pick-up food faster.*

   d. *Add a lighter late-evening menu, to be offered after the dinner rush is over.*

   e. *Have theme nights planned for normally slow nights.*

6. Implement the plans.

   a. *Establish a timetable for execution of plans.*

   b. *Advertise externally and promote internally.*

   c. *Start doing it.*

   d. *Keep careful records of results.*

   e. *Observe the good and bad points of what you are doing.*

   f. *Refine and adjust specific actions, as you go along.*

   g. *Reinforce the good features.*

   h. *Correct the flaws.*

7. Evaluate the results of your efforts.

   Decide whether to continue, modify or terminate the plan.

Successful marketing programs are based on in-depth knowledge of prospective customers' wants and needs. They include a broad range of tools, called "the marketing mix." Among the tools are market research, product and concept development, packaging, pricing, advertising, sales promotion and personal selling strategies.

Every Business Has a Life Cycle

Typical of all businesses, restaurants pass through a life cycle consisting of the following five stages. It is essential at each stage to know where you are because your marketing activities should be based on what is required at each particular stage.

Life Cycle Stage	Characteristics of that Stage
1. Introduction	Your restaurant has just been started. It is trying to survive and become established. Your systems are being perfected.
2. Conservative Growth	A period of slow and steady growth of sales as more people learn about your restaurant. New ideas are tried to attract more people.
3. Rapid Growth	Your reputation spreads. The word is out that you have a unique restaurant and serve good food and drinks. Your popularity grows rapidly, as do your sales. Competitors notice your success.
4. Leveled Maturity	Competition intensifies as others copy your ideas, and new competitors emerge. Growth ceases and you try to hold on to your share of the market.
5. Rejuvenation or Decline	Competitors and new entrants not only take your ideas but improve on them. You must reinvent your business by introducing new ideas that differentiate and position you ahead of the pack, or your restaurant's business will decline.

At first a restaurant focuses its advertising on letting the public know it exists, what it offers and where it is. Then its advertising changes to promotions that would bring in first-time patrons and increase the frequency of patronage by existing customers. After that, it would attempt to hold its market share by capitalizing on the reputation it built in the previous stages. It would remind people about its quality and the reasons it became popular. Finally, if it succeeded in rejuvenating itself, its advertising would emphasize what is new or improved and the whole process would start over.

Market Research Pays Off

The more you know about the people in your marketing area, the better you will be able to serve them. You will be aware of their customs and special holidays—when, where and how they spend their money, how you should price your menu, and what level of service will be expected of you.

There are three types of information about prospective customers that can help a restaurant plan a marketing strategy. They are:

1. Demographic information
2. Geographic information
3. Psychographic information

Demographics are facts about people, such as their age, income, education, occupation, race, religion, nationality. Geographic information tells you where people live and work. It will also tell you something about their dining and drinking patterns. For example, harried commuters are more apt to rush to their cars after work than in-town dwellers who might stop for cocktails or dinner.

Psychographic information can tell you such things as whether people are brand conscious, influenced by peer groups, socially oriented or have a need to keep up with others. Some persons are attracted to prestigious establishments where people of influence or celebrities are known to frequent. Psychrographics deal with lifestyles and motivational influences on people's spending behavior.

There are market research firms that sell market information to businesses. Their names are available at the reference department of your local library and in business and telephone directories.

If you cannot afford to purchase information, you can gather a great deal of it on your own through observation and discreet questioning. Public information agencies—such as chambers of commerce, state and city agencies, as well as newspapers and radio stations—can provide much information.

Check out your competition in addition to researching your prospective customers. It is also a good way to glean new ideas. The success of a competitor may, in some cases, be an indicator of how well you may do.

Investigate the economic trend of your community. Consider where is it headed; do not focus on what it was like in the past—conditions may change in the future. Your market research will influence decisions that may make or break you. Following is a list of questions that should be answered by your research:

1. Who are your competitors? What are they offering? Menu? Style of service? Entertainment? Atmosphere and decor?

2. Are they successful? What seems to make them successful?

3. What kinds of customers do they attract?

4. What special things are they doing to attract their clientele?

5. What are their merchandising and pricing policies?

6. What are their apparent strengths?

7. Do they have any weaknesses that you may capitalize on?

You cannot be sure your concept is truly unique until you research your competitors. Your research will also help you identify the merchandising styles to which particular segments of the market respond, and it may guide you to marketing strategies that will effectively reach your desired clientele. Beyond that, it will give you some idea of the degree of difficulty you can expect to encounter in your effort to penetrate the market.

Personal Research Is Valuable

The most direct way to gather information about your competitors is to patronize their restaurants. Don't be bashful about your research efforts; you can be sure they will be researching your business as soon as you open. Observe everything about them that may be of help to you. Chat with waitpeople. Question suppliers and delivery people. Talk to other business owners and anyone else who might give you valuable information. Everything you learn will help you develop a competitive strategy and capitalize on their weaknesses. Here are some things to look at when researching another establishment.

1. Kind of restaurant: its concept, style of service, type of clientele
2. Approximate seating capacity
3. Waiting time to be seated and to be served
4. Efficiency and friendliness of the host and waitperson
5. Number of menu offerings—food and beverages
6. Variety of offerings
7. Quality of food and drinks
8. Cost relative to quality
9. Arrangement of dining room and appearance of table settings
10. Atmosphere and decor of rooms
11. Apparent cleanliness of the facility
12. Availability of waitperson when needed
13. Smoke-free section for nonsmokers provided
14. Background music
15. General ambiance of establishment
16. Type of sales promotional techniques utilized—displays, price inducements, personal selling
17. Bill presented in a timely manner and correctly added
18. Payment collected quickly
19. Being thanked for your patronage

Know Your Target Market

Not everyone likes the same thing—people over 50 do not generally have the same taste for music or ambiance or even foods, as do people in their early twenties. Unfortunately, because restaurateurs want everyone to feel welcome in their establishment, many make the mistake of thinking their target market is "everyone." In fact, their target market is the segment of the population that strongly wants or needs what they offer and is most apt to patronize their establishment.

Most restaurants have a stronger following within certain demographic groups than they do within others. The best way to identify your target market is to segment the market according to demographic, geographic and psychographic variables (see Figure 11.1).

Recognize Your Customers' Wants and Needs

Observe the things your customers ask for when they come to your establishment and determine the things you can offer to satisfy their wants or needs.

Information can also be obtained by researching consumer trends and preferences in restaurant industry trade journals. Popularity indexes of food and drink preferences are periodically published.

Another resource is the National Restaurant Association which compiles data on customer spending patterns and other industry statistics. Their annual publication, entitled *Restaurant Industry Operations Report,* can provide valuable information on the performance of various kinds of foodservice establishments.

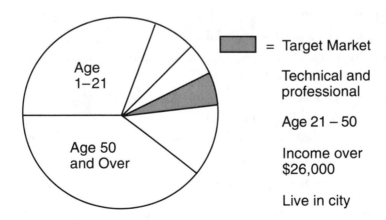

Figure 11.1: This diagram shows how a particular target market is segmented.

Catering to Separate Markets

Some restaurants have two distinct types of clientele—in the day-time they may cater to workers, shoppers and tourists, while at night they may cater to a social, fun-seeking clientele. With careful planning, you may be able to serve more than one type, provided they are acceptable to each other and your desired image is not compromised. The following example illustrates how customer wants and needs may be analyzed and satisfied.

Type of Guest	Want or Need	Response
Workers, lunchtime	Nourishment	Offer good, healthy food
Workers, after work	Relaxation	Offer comfortable seating, soft music
Dinner guests	Excitement	Offer interesting food and drinks
Entertainment seekers	Stimulation	Offer high-energy music and dancing
Social guests	Meet people	Offer an informal lounge atmosphere, with close, comfortable seating and stand-up bars

Strategies for Meeting the Competition

There are three types of competitive strategies you may consider when starting out—market penetration, differentiation and concentration.

The *market penetration strategy* is one by which you penetrate the market with lower prices than your competitors. This is an often used strategy, but it is feasible only when accompanied by tight cost controls in all expense areas, which allow you to make a profit even though you charge lower prices.

The *differentiation strategy*, which refers to setting your business apart from your competitors, differentiates your business by stressing such things as its uniqueness or higher quality in your advertising. Uniqueness can take many forms. A restaurant's unusual atmosphere and decor, music, specialized style of service or menu offerings can differentiate it from its competitors.

You can also make your restaurant appear to be different, simply by the way you position your competitors in your advertising. An example of this would be the following statement in an advertisement: "Have It Both Ways—Now You Can Enjoy Healthy Dining in a Smoke-Free Environment." If your competitors allow smoking everywhere and offer only deep-fried foods, your restaurant would appear quite different to your target market.

Concentration is a strategy that involves focusing on a particular customer group or geographic location or style of service. While the cost-based and differentiation strategies are aimed at the entire potential market, the concentration strategy aims at a particular need of a specific segment of your target market.

The Secret to Growth—Getting New Customers

Some customers may come to your restaurant because it is the newest place in town. Others will come because you are close by or because they have heard good things about it. Many more will intend to come someday but will never get around to doing so, unless you do something special to draw them in.

Researchers have found that consumers go through a decision-making process before making purchases. Restaurant patrons, knowingly or unknowingly, pass through the same five stages. The process may be depicted as follows:

1. Awareness—this is when a person first realizes your restaurant exists.

2. Interest—develops when they hear something good about your place from a friend or see an enticing advertisement.

3. Evaluation—occurs as they mull over what they have seen or heard and either decide to try it sometime or forget it.

4. Trial—takes place when the customer visits your restaurant to see if he or she likes it.

5. Adoption or Rejection—is what results, depending on whether the customer is pleased or not by their first experience at your establishment.

It is important to understand a consumer's decision-making process because it reflects how hard it is to get new customers and it points out the importance of taking good care of your present customers.

New customers are your key to growth. To get them, you must make people aware of your existence through creative advertising and sales promotion programs aimed at first-time customers. You can also gain new customers by doing an exceptional job with your present customers—satisfying them so well that they will tell their friends about your restaurant. Without question, the most effective form of advertising is word-of-mouth.

How To Make the Most of Your Grand Opening

People are attracted to grand openings because they represent something new, exciting, perhaps a better deal. A grand opening is a very important time for a restaurant to do things right. This is when it can really impress new customers. Unfortunately, many establishments waste the opportunity to cash in on their grand opening and, in some cases, do such a poor job that it takes months to recover from an initial flurry of bad word-of-mouth advertising. Here are some ways to make a grand opening successful.

1. Carefully preplan a schedule of preliminary activities to assure you will be ready on the designated date of the grand opening. Do not have your grand opening until you are ready to do everything right.

2. Thoroughly train your staff prior to the grand opening.

3. Make sure all equipment is assembled properly, cleaned and tested. This should be done adequately in advance to allow tradespeople time to come back and make corrections if necessary.

4. Be certain all of your licenses and permits will be issued, before the grand opening date is announced. More than one opening has had to be postponed because of a last-minute snag. Work closely with the licensing authorities.

5. Communicate regularly with your suppliers to make certain their deliveries will arrive in advance to avoid distractions,

back-orders or returned merchandise during the grand opening.

6. Schedule a dry-run party before going public with your grand opening. A dry run is a private function to which you invite your relatives and close friends, business associates and anyone who can ever do you any good, such as media people, suppliers, politicians, liquor, fire and health authorities, lenders, investors, and contractors.

    You can expect a high rate of attendance because the event is free. This is a chance to strut your stuff in a friendly atmosphere, but even though no one will complain (because the price is right), if something goes wrong, every detail including mistakes and problems should be handled as though the people were paying. The reason for having a dry-run party is to iron out any wrinkles in your operation.

The best planned grand opening will be of little value if people do not know about it. So, you must advertise and publicize it well in advance in order for people to talk it up with their friends. A frequently used technique for announcing grand openings with a big splash is to have all of your contractors and suppliers sponsor a full page newspaper advertisement that congratulates you on your opening and wishes you well. The contractors have made money on you and your suppliers will make a lot in the future if you are successful—so it is in their best interest to do this. Besides, it puts their name in the public's eye, since most ads of this type have the sponsors business cards arranged as a border around the perimeter of the ad. Everybody wins.

Other things that can be done to announce a grand opening are:

1. Visit nearby businesses to introduce yourself to their owners. In addition, make yourself known to their employees, since retail store clerks are frequently asked for recommendations on a place to eat by their customers.

2. Offer an introductory discount to employees of neighboring businesses.

3. Mail a copy of your menu and information about your hours and facilities to all businesses within your dominant marketing area. Be sure to emphasize your name and address prominently

so that if the recipient does not read the entire mailing, they will at least know who you are and where you are.

4. Supply all visitor information centers in your community with literature about your restaurant to be displayed in their racks. Give a gift certificate for a free lunch to the person at the visitor information center who dispenses information to visitors.

5. Put an eye-catching "Coming Soon" sign in your front window announcing the date of the grand opening. This should be done well in advance to attract the attention of the most people possible.

Free Publicity Can Be Yours for the Asking

Newspaper editors who have the responsibility of filling many pages with print welcome newsworthy publicity articles from businesses. On slow news days, press releases are heavily utilized.

Publicity articles can be about a wide variety of things, such as grand openings, new products, significant contributions to charities, awards from professional associations, a change of name or a promotion of a key person. They must be of genuine interest to the public and cannot be blatantly self-serving, contain unsubstantiated claims or be critical of other products. In short, they cannot be advertisements. But, if they are truly newsworthy and well written and submitted on time, they stand an excellent chance of being published.

Free publicity is more valuable than paid advertising because readers tend to believe news articles much more than advertisements. Most people do not realize publicity articles are usually written by the business that they are about. They are thought to have been written by an unbiased person and therefore must be true.

Photographs make publicity articles much more interesting and increase their chances of being placed in a good location in a newspaper. They increase the readership rate dramatically and editors like to run them. To be used, however, they must be of good reproduction quality. It is worth trading a meal and a couple of drinks to have a professional photographer take a picture for you.

Following are some tips for writing successful publicity articles:

1. Submit time-sensitive articles adequately in advance of the paper's deadline. Find out your local newspaper's deadlines for copy.

2. Send articles to the appropriate editor. For example, an article announcing a promotion in your organization should be sent to the business editor, while an article announcing the sponsorship of a softball team by your restaurant should be sent to the sports editor.

3. Articles should be typed, double-spaced on plain white paper. However, if you have a really important newsworthy story that cannot wait, telephone the editor.

4. Summarize the Who, Why, What, When and Where of the story in the first paragraph. Then proceed to give the details in subsequent paragraphs. This is done so that if a person reads only the first paragraph, they will at least know your name and the important facts.

5. In the case of a longer story, let the editor know if the article was written exclusively for his or her paper.

6. If an article is not time-sensitive, indicate it is being "submitted for publication on a space available basis." This gives it a greater chance of being published when space becomes available.

7. Run a paid advertisement (preferably with a photograph) on the same page that the publicity article appears. You can make claims and self-serving statements in your ad and the credibility given to the publicity article will tend to transfer to what is said in the paid ad, thereby giving it greater acceptance.

It pays to relate well to your community—become involved with civic groups and projects. If public speaking is something you enjoy, that is a good way to gain favorable exposure. Many groups are constantly looking for interesting speakers and would love to have a presentation on cooking, wines, beers or a tour of your restaurant. It is a good way to make acquaintances, elevate the image of your establishment and get additional publicity because speaking events are often announced by the sponsoring group in a press release.

Give Customers Reasons To Come Back

Special attention gives customers a feeling of being appreciated and makes them want to come back soon. There are many ways to give special attention to customers. A friendly greeting when they arrive and a thank-you when they leave makes their visit much more personal. This is especially effective when done by the manager—everyone likes to know the manager.

Table tents and lobby posters that announce future events, such as New Year's Eve and Mothers' Day or dinner/theater combination packages, can be effective tools in bringing people back.

Theme nights are very successful in some restaurants, particularly where customers are given the opportunity to participate in events. Listed below is a collection of ideas for theme nights. Some are straightforward, such as holiday observances, and others require a creative flair and the right setting to do them. But all of them will stimulate your creativity and lead you to other ideas. Consider all of the possibilities associated with themes—contests, prizes, special music, costumes and decorations.

Special Events and Theme Suggestions

Salute to the Armed Forces	Hockey Games
Calypso Beach Party	Basketball Games
Old Time Hollywood Night	Sidewalk Sales
Après Ski	Carnival Day
New Year's Day	St. Patrick's Day
Super Bowl Day	April Fool's Day
Homecoming Weekend	Easter
Olympics	Mother's Day
Labor Day	Father's Day
Back to College Days	Graduation Day
Columbus Day	Independence Day
Veteran's Day	Cajun Festival
Football Day	Washington's Birthday
Thanksgiving Day	Lincoln's Birthday
Christmas Day	Fashion Show
Mardi Gras	Art Exhibit

Patriot's Day	Opera Night
May Day	Country Fair
Dollar Days	Halloween Party
Theater Night	Marathon Mania
Baseball Party	Chinese New Year
Kentucky Derby	Hawaiian Cruise
Gay Nineties	Sing Along
Roaring Twenties	Election Day Party
Wine Tastings	Sadie Hawkins' Day
Cabaret Night	Mystery Dinner
Masked Ball	Chicago 1920s
Cartoon Night	Soap Opera Night

Acquiring Your Desired Image

How do you want to be perceived? The answer to this question will direct your advertising, merchandising, sales promotion and publicity activities. Once you decide how you want the public to view your restaurant, you must scrutinize every activity you conduct to be certain it clearly signals that image.

The hard- or soft-sell message of your ads, your choice of radio stations, the tone of your advertisements—all transmit an image of your business. If they are not well thought out to convey the precise image you want, you may be wasting your money. Advertising budgets for restaurants typically range from 2 percent to 3 percent of sales (however, some are as low as 0 percent and others as high as 5 percent).

It is important for everyone in your organization to have a clear understanding of what your desired image is and to work to achieve it—particularly service employees, who are at the point of contact with your customers.

Should You Advertise?

Advertising has become a fact of life in the business world. People expect it, look for it and, in spite of its many abuses, still place a great deal of trust in it. There are many reasons to advertise restaurants. The most common reasons are listed below:

1. To introduce a new restaurant
2. To attract new customers
3. To test new ideas
4. To let the public know what you are doing
5. To announce special holiday and theme events
6. To publicize a new or changed menu
7. To position your establishment a certain way
8. To reposition your competition
9. To resell lost customers
10. To introduce a new management
11. To report your achievements to the public
12. To create and maintain a certain image
13. To increase sales
14. To keep your name in the public's eye, particularly if your competitors advertise
15. To stimulate conversation and word-of-mouth advertising

Effective Use of Advertising Media

Every year, a great deal of money is wasted on advertising by restaurants desperately seeking to reach new customers. Many ads are poorly written or placed in inferior locations in newspapers, and radio commercials are often aired on the wrong stations. An ad has to be run in the newspaper or on the radio or television station that is read or listened to by the target market. It also has to be run at the right times and in the right position. For example, the inside, lower corner of a newspaper page is a poor location for a small ad because many people read newspapers while sitting with their legs crossed and drape the paper across their lap. Consequently they rarely see the ads in the lower, inside corners of their paper.

Frequency is important in advertising. The chances of a reader noticing an ad that is run one time is pure luck. If an ad is run regularly, the chances of it being seen are much greater. In general, it is better to run a smaller size ad more often than to run a larger size ad just once. This is especially true with radio advertising, where the listener has no opportunity to cut out and save a commercial. Figure 11.2 is a list of media accompanied by some of the advantages and disadvantages of each.

Figure 11.2: Media Analysis

Media Analysis

RADIO

Advantages

- Easy to target market through choice of station
- Captive audience during drive times
- 99 percent of homes are said to have radios
- 95 percent of all cars are said to have radios

Disadvantages

- Audio only; can't save or cut out
- Lacks visual appeal

NEWSPAPERS

Advantages

- Timely, contain news of the day
- Easy to change on short notice
- Published frequently
- Can tie in advertisements with local events
- Less expensive than magazines and broadcast media

Disadvantages

- Short life, usually discarded daily
- Ads may get buried among many others

Figure 11.2, *continued.*

- Some people read certain sections only
- Not as well read on certain days
- Not well-suited for high-quality photos

TELEVISION

Advantages

- Has both audio and visual appeal
- Easy to target market through choice of program
- Can be heard from another room without viewing
- Widely viewed in most households

Disadvantages

- Relatively more expensive
- Longer time required to produce commercials
- Remotes allow muting out of commercials
- VCRs allow fast-forwarding through commercials
- Better-quality commercials that utilize professional actors must be produced by a specialized production company
- Can't be saved as with print media (unless taped)

MAGAZINES

Advantages

- Can be highly targeted to demographic groups, geographic areas, particular lifestyles and special interests
- Have a long life, may be saved
- May have multiple readers, are shared and reread
- May lend prestige to advertiser

Figure 11.2, *continued*.

- Better-quality paper allows high-quality photos

Disadvantages
- Advertiser may pay for wasted circulation outside of the restaurant's marketing area
- Require long lead times up to several months
- May be expensive

BILLBOARDS **Advantages**
- Useful for giving directions
- Good for reminder ads

Disadvantages
- Viewers limited mainly to motorists
- Not allowed in certain locations
- Can only accommodate short messages

CAR CARDS **Advantages**
- Can be located very precisely
- Most effective in mass transportation vehicles

Disadvantages
- Useful only for short messages or reminder ads
- Viewers are largely limited to riders

HANDBILLS **Advantages**
- Relatively inexpensive to produce
- Can be targeted easily
- Can contain coupons and be saved

Disadvantages
- Considered junk mail by some people

Figure 11.2, *continued.*

- Must be very catchy or they are thrown away
- May create backlash if they cause littering

DIRECT MAIL **Advantages**

- Computerized mailing lists available
- Can be personalized
- Highly selective; good targeting is possible
- Can be saved or passed on to others
- Can include coupons

Disadvantages

- Low percentage of return, usually under 5 percent
- Very expensive
- Often thrown out as junk mail

Establishing Realistic Sales Goals

It is easy for enthusiastic entrepreneurs to overestimate sales. This is very risky in the restaurant business because all other budgeted cost and expense projections are based on sales—exaggerated sales can delude a planner into budgeting more funds for expenses than should have been allocated and may lead to a loss on operations.

There are many approaches to setting sales goals, but the best approach is to use a combination of several methods and temper it with your own gut feeling. Industry sources, such as the National Restaurant Association's *Annual Restaurant Operations Report,* can give you typical sales figures for various types of establishments. The figures are expressed in total dollar amounts as well as sales per seat. Trade journals also conduct surveys and publish useful information. These are all good numbers to use as cross-references, but you should calculate your own figures based on your seating capacity, expected turnovers meal by meal and day by day and average guest check.

Following is an illustration of one method for estimating sales:

Step 1: Estimate the *number of customers* you expect to patronize your establishment during each meal period, for each day of the week.

	Mon.	Tue.	Wed.	Thur.	Fri.	Sat.	Sun.	Total
Lunch	75	75	80	90	100	90	80	590
Dinner	35	45	60	65	85	90	75	455
Bar Only	20	25	40	50	65	70	25	295

Total Customers per Week   1340

Step 2: Calculate the *average menu price* for each category of items on your menu. (A weighted average that takes into account the popularity and sales of each item, in comparison to the others, is best. But, until you are in business for a while and have a sales history, this simple average method will suffice.)

Sandwiches and Salads	$ 4.75
Entrees	10.95
Desserts	2.50
Drinks	2.75

Step 3: Determine the amount of an *average guest check* by estimating what a typical guest will be apt to order. (If you expect that only one out of every two guests will order a drink or a salad, you may indicate the item as .5 salad or .5 drinks. This will keep your estimate on the conservative side.)

Lunch	Sandwich or Salad plus .5 Drinks	$ 6.13
Dinner	Entree, Salad, .5 Dessert, plus 2 Drinks	22.45
Bar Only	Average 2 Drinks	5.50

Step 4: Multiply your average guest check by the number of customers expected per week to determine your *estimated weekly sales.*

590 lunch customers	×	$ 6.13	=	$ 3,617
455 dinner customers	×	22.45	=	10,215
295 bar only customers	×	5.50	=	1,623
		Total Weekly Sales		**$15,455**

Step 5: Finally, multiply your estimated weekly sales by 52 to arrive at your estimated annual sales.

$$52 \text{ weeks} \times \$15,455 = \$803,660$$

The benefit of this process is it tailors your sales objective to your specific business and local conditions. The resultant annual sales figure may then be compared to industry averages.

Tips for Achieving Sales Goals

1. Be prepared for the rush season and the busy periods. Have your staff fully trained and your equipment in peak condition. That is the secret to maximizing sales. Take advantage of the opportunities when they are there—be ready to handle a crowd.

2. Believe in yourself and set high standards—serve good food and beverages, keep your establishment clean and attractive. Offer a good value for the prices you charge and you will soon get valuable word-of-mouth advertising from your customers.

3. Keep a positive attitude. All months are not created equal and there will be slow times. You can offset slow periods to some degree by being creative and coming up with sales promotional ideas that "keep smoke in the chimneys," but your main focus should be on maximizing your sales when people feel like coming out and are ready to spend their money.

4. Let your customers know you care about them. Establish a rapport with them. That way, if they have a complaint some night you will be able to handle it without their becoming resentful toward you.

5. Get feedback from your customers. Listen to their compliments and their complaints—they are telling you what they like and don't like.

6. Never embarrass a customer for mispronouncing the name of a menu item or a wine. Be sympathetic and helpful—do not ever diminish them in any way.

Ways To Increase Food and Beverage Sales

The three basic purposes of a menu are (1) to let customers know what you offer, (2) to let them know how much things cost and (3) to promote the sale of certain highly profitable items.

Sales may be enhanced by bringing certain items to the attention of customers. Boxing an item makes it stand out on a menu (see Figure 11.3).

The location of items on a menu can affect their sales. Knowing this, you can place certain high-profit items in strategic places where they are apt to be selected more often. Studies have shown that people's eyes tend to follow certain patterns when reading menus (see Figure 11.4).

```
Downeast
LobsterBake

   Maine Lobster,
   Steamed  Clams,
   Corn on the Cob,
Sausage, Boiled Egg &
 Onion, Baked Beans
   and Watermelon

 Only $22.00
```

Figure 11.3: Boxing an item on a menu emphasizes it.

	Menu	
3rd Spot		2nd Spot
	First spot to be seen	
4th Spot		Last Spot

Figure 11.4: A typical reading pattern for a threefold menu.

Waitpeople should be taught the art of suggestive selling. When done in an informational manner it can be very helpful to customers. Some helpful hints for increasing sales are:

1. Reduce confusion in customers' minds by using menu descriptions that clearly describe food items and wines.

2. Make it easy for people to order. Assign numbers to wines, and, where it fits into the style of service of a restaurant, the same can be done for entrees. This gives customers the opportunity to order by number if they cannot pronounce the name of an item.

3. Use large type sizes. It makes names seem less intimidating to inexperienced diners and assists people with visual impairments.

4. Print menus on white or light-colored stock for easy reading. The covers of a wine menu should coordinate with the colors of the decor and the mood of the atmosphere.

5. Use menus that are appropriate to your table sizes. Oversized and odd-shaped ones can be cumbersome on a crowded table top and may annoy guests.

6. Proofread menus and wine lists carefully before approving them for printing, especially when they include foreign names and terms.

Some restaurants use contests and incentive plans to stimulate waitpeople to promote certain items to guests. Table tents and menu clip-ons can also be used to highlight specialties. A successful tactic for increasing wine sales in small, upscale restaurants is to place an unopened bottle of wine on each table and include wine glasses in the table setting. If the guests do not wish to order wine, the glasses are removed. Displaying a wine rack in the restaurant lobby has also proven to be a successful way to increase wine sales.

Don't Forget Telephone Selling

Phone calls are less costly and faster to make than personal visits. Telephone selling is an excellent way to notify the business community of your function rooms and banquet packages. They can be used to solicit a variety of bookings—such as retirement parties, holiday and birthday parties, promotion parties, sales meetings and awards presentation meetings. The telephone blitz works best when followed up with a sales packet and a personal letter that reviews the content of the call.

A significant amount of interest in your restaurant can be raised with a carefully planned and tested telephone message. It is essential however that a telephone sales script contain all of the basic elements of a personal sales call, namely:

- a brief introduction that tells the listener who you are and the purpose of your call,

- an attention getting statement that gives the listener a reason for continuing to listen,

- a discussion of the features and benefits you're offering,

- an opportunity for the listener to ask questions or voice any objections, and

- an appeal for an action of some sort or a personal meeting.

Action Guidelines

✔ Develop a seven-step marketing plan for a new restaurant.

✔ Describe in a detailed paragraph the identifying characteristics of your target market.

✔ Write a press release announcing the grand opening of your restaurant.

✔ Plan an advertising campaign, based on 3 percent of your estimated sales, allocating the funds among the media you select.

✔ Make a list of the people you would invite to your dry-run party.

✔ Prepare a timetable for the marketing tasks that will lead to your grand opening.

SANITATION, SAFETY AND RESPONSIBILITY

A restaurant serves its customers best when it serves them responsibly. As a manager you have responsibilities that extend beyond the bottom line of your income statement—you hold a public trust to serve wholesome food in a safe establishment and to dispense alcoholic beverages in a prudent manner. There are three areas of concern that restaurant managers should keep informed of and monitor closely; they are food sanitation, safety and responsible service of alcoholic beverages.

What Is Food Sanitation?

In common parlance, the term *food sanitation* refers to all activities and conditions that insure safe and wholesome food will be delivered to restaurant patrons. It includes employee hygiene and work habits, food preparation, holding equipment and the physical facilities of a restaurant—all in addition to the food supply itself.

Purchasing Food

An effective sanitation program starts with good purchasing practices. Restaurants must buy commercially produced products from reliable vendors who in turn acquire their food supplies from food packing and processing plants that are inspected and adhere to specified health standards.

When you start out in the restaurant business, you will have to select the purveyors from which you will buy. It is advisable to interview several of them in each food category to find out what their policies are and how they handle their products and rotate stock. Visit their establishment to see how clean and orderly it is. Prices are important but should not be your only determinant when choosing suppliers.

Receiving Shipments

The receiving function in your restaurant is also an important point in a good sanitation program. Every shipment of food should be checked for broken packages, dented or swollen cans, proper color and stage of maturity, as well as proper temperature of the product. Frozen and refrigerated products should be delivered in vehicles that hold them at the proper temperature. The latter is especially critical for fish and poultry products which are highly perishable.

Storing Food

Once inspected and signed for, food should be put into the proper storage location immediately. Frozen products should be put away first, followed by refrigerated products and finally dry storage products. It is advisable to check your freezer and walk-in refrigerator thermometers periodically to make sure they are keeping the proper temperatures. If they are inaccurate, they should be calibrated by a refrigeration technician.

To prevent contamination while in refrigeration, raw products should be stored on lower shelves, below cooked products—and items that may drip should be wrapped tightly and placed on lower shelves, as well. All foods in storage should be raised off the floor. Dry storage rooms should be dry, dark, and preferably cool. The following are recommended temperatures for refrigerated storage of certain food groups:

Product	Temperature	Humidity
Meat and poultry	32 to 36°F	75 to 85%
Fish	30 to 34°F	75 to 85%
Dairy products	38 to 40°F	75 to 85%
Most fruits and vegetables	40 to 45°F	85 to 95%

Food Handling

The food handling phase is the part of the process that requires constant training and supervision by management. Employees must be taught the basics of food spoilage and contamination. Several excellent courses on food sanitation are available on tape from the National Restaurant Association and the National Institute for the Foodservice Industry. Local health inspectors can be very helpful when developing training programs for employees. See *State Administrative Officials Classified by Function 1993–94* in your local library for state health department addresses.

Serving Food

The holding and serving stage is critical because cooked food should not be held on the serving line for long periods of time. It is recommended that food be cooked in smaller batches and that the serving line be resupplied periodically. This not only cuts down on the amount of time the food is held, it also tends to reduce the amount of leftovers at the end of each shift. Someone should check the serving line with an instant-read thermometer every day to make sure hot foods are being kept hot, over 140°F, and cold foods are being kept cold, 41°F or lower, while on the serving line.

Cleaning and Sanitizing

The proper cleaning and sanitizing of equipment is another vital component of an effective sanitation program. Training must be ongoing for dishwashers because of the high turnover rate in that job. Detergent salespeople are excellent resources for dish-washing machine training—they want you to continue using their products so most of the companies will supply you with audio visual aids and do demonstrations for you on request. The dish-washing function should receive constant supervision to control dish breakage, as well.

For proper dish-washing, soiled ware should be prescraped and loaded neatly into dish racks to insure that they will be washed thoroughly. Dishes and utensils should be washed with water of 140°F to 160°F and sanitized with water of 180°F. Clean dishes should be stored quickly at their point of next use, to reduce the chances of their contamination by unwashed hands.

Dealing with Pests

Pest control can be a difficult problem in many inner-city locations, because pests are a community problem. You may operate a very clean establishment, but insects and rodents may be all around you in the neighborhood. They can enter your premises through open doors or cracks in walls or floors, or they may come in on the food products and supplies that you buy. The most effective way to deal with pests is to contract a professional exterminator to deal with the problem on a continuous basis. You should also seal off any points of entry that you can locate. An ongoing preventative program should be worked out with the exterminator.

Planning for Good Sanitation

Much can be done when you are building or renovating a restaurant to facilitate a sound sanitation program, such as choosing easily cleanable floor and wall materials, equipment and work surfaces. Foodservice equipment should bear the NSF label on it—the label signifies that the equipment design was inspected and found to meet the standards of the National Sanitation Foundation.

Another aspect of planning for good sanitation is providing the necessary tools and cleaning supplies, and assigning responsibility for cleaning certain work areas and equipment to particular individuals.

Employee Safety

The true costs of accidents in the workplace often go unnoticed. Aside from the pain inflicted on an injured person, there is the loss of the employee's skills, medical costs, a possible increase in the restaurant's worker's compensation rate and a loss of morale if accidents occur frequently.

Most accidents can be attributed to unsafe acts, unsafe equipment or unsafe working conditions. In a restaurant kitchen, the most common accidents are cuts, burns and falls. All of these can be prevented with proper training, proper equipment and proper supervision, but management must first be aware of the potential hazards. The causes of the problems must be identified and solutions to each must be developed. This can be done by conducting a hazard analysis of the facility—and inspecting it from one end to the other.

Management must provide safe equipment with protective guards and other safety features; then the employees must be taught how to properly use the equipment and how to perform their manual duties safely. It is useful to post safety procedures near any piece of potentially hazardous equipment to remind employees of the possible dangers if misused.

Customer Safety

Patrons will not return to establishments that are unsafe. It is important when evaluating your customer safety program to walk through the entire dining process that a customer experiences when they patronize your establishment—starting in your driveway. Following is a partial list of things you should evaluate:

- Is your driveway well marked?
- Is your parking lot well lighted?
- Are parking spaces adequately sized and clearly painted?
- Has snow been removed, and have ice patches been sanded?
- Are there any loose steps or otherwise unsafe stairs?
- Are there any carpets torn or loose?
- Are any tables or chairs weak or damaged?
- Have cracked dishes or glassware been removed from service?
- Are emergency exits clearly marked with lighted signs?
- Are your servers' practices such that they protect guests from accidental spills?
- Do you have safety procedures in place to handle emergencies?

Fire Safety

The most common type of restaurant fires are grease fires in exhaust hoods. Ordinances in most communities require that fire suppressant equipment be installed in restaurant kitchens, but such equipment does not prevent fires. Regular cleaning of equipment and duct work, where grease can build up and become heated to ignitable temperatures, is the only way to prevent this type of fire.

The next most common fires are electrically caused. Electrical fires can be best avoided by training employees how to handle electrical equipment. Teaching them such things as to not pull cords from wall receptacles by yanking on the cord (but rather to grasp the plug) and to turn off equipment when it is not going to be used for quite a while help a great deal. Employees should be taught how to use the various types of fire extinguishers and to immediately report any defective electrical equipment.

Alcohol Responsibility

Not all restaurants need to serve alcoholic beverages—it depends on the market niche you wish to occupy. Although it is estimated that 70 percent of the adult population drinks alcoholic beverages to some degree, one may safely assume that very few people would want a drink at breakfast time. Therefore, alcohol service should be considered in the context of the wants and needs of your desired clientele.

Where alcohol service is feasible, it can be a significant profit center, provided the bar operations are controlled well and service is rendered responsibly. Dram shop laws and negligence statutes place a formidable responsibility on proprietors of alcoholic beverage establishments.

Know the Signs of Intoxication

All servers of alcohol should be trained to look for signs that indicate the state of a customer's sobriety. The challenge to a server is not to "shut off" a person after they have consumed too much, but rather to help them drink in such a way that they will have an enjoyable time without becoming intoxicated. The following four stages can be considered as signs on the course of becoming intoxicated. If a server can recognize the characteristics of each sign, he or she will be able to intervene to slow down the customer's rate of consumption as necessary.

1. Lessening of inhibitions
2. Exercising poor judgment
3. Displaying an impairment of reaction time
4. Exhibiting a loss of coordination

People tend to relax when they have a drink, their *inhibitions lessen.* As a result, they may act differently—some turn quiet while others become talkative, but all are relaxing in their own way. People can drink for quite a while without becoming intoxicated if they drink at a slow enough pace and do not consume more alcohol than their liver can metabolize per hour (one ounce or less, depending on body size).

The next noticeable affect of intoxication is *exercising poor judgment.* This occurs when a person drinks too fast. Their blood alcohol content rises and they begin to do things that they probably would not do if they were not under the influence of alcohol. They might irritate other customers by making loud outbursts of laughter or off-color remarks, becoming argumentative, chug-a-lugging or ordering doubles in rapid succession.

Further drinking leads to a *loss of reactions.* That stage of intoxication is reflected by such traits as slurring speech, fumbling with money or cigarettes and being unable to concentrate. At that point the drinker's brain and motor skills are not synchronized.

The last stage, *loss of coordination,* is exhibited by stumbling and weaving, spilling drinks and dropping money, falling asleep and a general inability to function normally.

It is in the last two stages that a drinker can do serious harm to him or herself and to others, so it is very important to prevent drinkers from entering those stages. This can be done by intervening with strategies that will slow a drinker's consumption rate. Servers should be aware of the conditions that influence the speed with which drinkers may become intoxicated and should take precautions to prevent their intoxication.

Following are some of those conditions:

- Drinking too fast
- Repeatedly ordering strong drinks
- Taking medications while drinking

- Drinking on an empty stomach
- Drinking when depressed, stressed or exhausted

In general, females have more fatty cells than males and tend to be smaller in body size. For those reasons, they tend to absorb alcohol into their bloodstream faster than males. In the same manner, a small male will be affected faster by his blood alcohol content than will a large male.

When servers are aware of a drinker's need to be slowed down, they can intervene by serving snacks that do not create thirst and by not asking for reorders right away. When done tactfully, the customer may not even realize what is happening.

Responsible Business Practices

A great deal has been done by state agencies, the TIPS (Training for Intervention Procedures by Servers of Alcohol) program, the National Restaurant Association and the major brewers and distillers of alcoholic beverages to educate the restaurant industry on the need for responsible business practices.

Licensees and servers of alcoholic beverages cannot eliminate their liability in issues involving alcohol, but they can certainly reduce their risk by establishing and adhering to responsible business practices, such as:

1. Conducting periodic, in-house training sessions on alcohol responsibility.
2. Letting their customers know what their policies are. Putting up posters and spelling out their policies on table tents, menus and wine lists.
3. Checking the ID of anyone who does not appear to be at least 30 years old. This allows a comfortable margin of safety, as opposed to trying to determine if a person is 21 years old.
4. Making sure all servers are acquainted with the restaurant's policies and practice them.
5. Keeping a list of all the things the bar does to abide by the law, such as conducting training sessions and checking IDs.

6. Keeping an incident log at the bar into which bartenders and servers enter a record of any situations where they had to shut off someone or refuse to serve a person.

7. Not soliciting refills until the customer asks for one.

8. Setting a limit on the number of stronger drinks that may be served to a person or developing recipes for weaker versions of those drinks.

9. Sending your servers to training programs such as the TIPS program.

10. Not having happy hours or similar programs that encourage people to consume excessive amounts of alcohol in short periods of time.

11. Making nonalcoholic drinks available.

12. Staffing adequately for peak periods so that servers can check IDs without being rushed and can monitor their customers properly.

13. Controlling the level of the lighting and music so that it does not encourage rapid drinking.

14. Offering free snacks to slow down consumption rates.

15. Offering free coffee to departing customers.

16. Calling taxicabs or arranging for safe transportation.

These kinds of activities establish you as a prudent, law abiding business person that runs an ethical establishment with well-trained employees and high standards. Consequently, they can contribute very positively to a legal defense, should one ever become necessary.

Liquor Laws

If you sell alcohol, you should abide by the spirit and the letter of the liquor laws. The alcoholic beverage control agency of each state publishes its regulations, which are based on the statutes of that state. A copy of the regulations may be obtained by writing to or calling the agency. The laws and regulations vary from state to state, but two things are common throughout the 50 states and the District of Columbia.

1. You cannot legally serve a minor. For the purposes of drinking, a minor is defined as any person under 21 years of age.

2. You cannot legally serve a person who is visibly intoxicated.

Checking IDs

It is imperative for a server of alcohol to check the ID of any person of questionable age. An ID Checking Guide may be purchased from the Drivers License Guide Company (415-369-4849). The publication describes in detail the specific features of driver's licenses of every state.

Following are some useful tips for checking the ID cards of persons of doubtful age:

1. Hold the card in your hand. Do not check it in a wallet. It is easier to see and feel imperfections when you hold a license.

2. Compare the picture on the ID with the face of the person. Pay particular attention to the mouth and chin.

3. Check the date of birth on the card and ask the person what it is?

4. Examine the card for signs of tampering. Feel the surface and look for discolorations, white-outs or erasures.

5. Check the thickness of the card to determine if the picture has been substituted.

6. Refer to the ID Checking Guide for out of state licenses.

Determining Who Is Visibly Intoxicated

Few laws stipulate the standards for determining "visible intoxication." It is therefore important for servers to be trained to recognize the signs of intoxication discussed earlier and to always act as would a prudent person who is guided by the intention to obey the law.

Action Guidelines

✔ Order a food sanitation code book from the public health agency of your state.

✔ If you plan to serve alcoholic beverages, order a liquor law book from the Alcoholic Beverage Control agency of your state.

✔ Obtain a list of food sanitation and safety practices from your local health inspector.

✔ Develop a list of responsible business practices and prepare a policy manual for your bar and servers.

✔ Create an outline for a training session on sanitation and safety for kitchen employees and another one on responsible beverage service for your bar employees and dining room servers.

Chapter
13

IF YOU SUCCEED—WHAT NEXT?

Some restaurants become an immediate success—those rare occurrences are usually the result of being in the right place at the right time with a unique concept that is well received by the target market. Most new restaurant ventures are not so lucky as to have all of those crucial factors intersect at the same time. For them success comes slowly as the result of much hard work, experimentation and concerted management.

If your restaurant survives the first five years, it is quite likely it will continue to flourish provided you remain enthusiastic about it and adhere to the sound business principles that enabled you to succeed in the first place. However, when a new business stabilizes and gives indications that it can continue to flourish, some people begin to tire of it. They discover that their main satisfaction came from building the business and not from operating it on a day-to-day basis. The question for them becomes, What next?

Whether or not a restaurateur continues to be enthralled with the business, a number of questions will inevitably surface. Should you sell the business and enjoy the fruits of your labor? Or should you stay as you are and continue to enjoy the business that you like? Should you expand? If you are highly successful, you might ponder the question, Should I franchise? Many chains have started from humble beginnings and have grown to national proportions. Drive down any miracle mile and count the success stories.

To decide what the right thing is for you to do, you will have to go back to square one—redefine your goals and evaluate the options. You will also need to consider the sacrifices required by each option and the implications on your lifestyle before you decide whether or not it is for you.

Should You Stay the Same?

Changes are constantly occurring in the restaurant field, new foods come into vogue, technology changes, consumer tastes change, economic conditions vacillate and new trends emerge. A restaurant must respond to change if it is going to survive over the long run. Few businesses are able to remain the same.

The trick is to be able to incorporate changes without sacrificing the concepts that initially made the restaurant successful. Managing change is said to be the biggest challenge most businesses will face as we approach the next century.

Should You Expand?

All restaurants should at least consider expansion when they initially start up. It is unfortunate when a business has to move because it outgrows its present location. One never knows if the dynamics that worked so well in the original setting will happen again in another location. Customers sometimes resent change and will try a competitor before following a business—if the competitor treats them well, they will probably not return.

The question of expansion has two facets: (1) should you and (2) can you? It may appear from your growth pattern that you should expand, but do you have the physical space to enlarge your operations? If you add on to your building, can you add on to your parking lot? How would the additional space integrate with your existing production system and flow of traffic? Can new equipment be placed where it is most needed?

Sometimes, when a restaurant cannot expand at its present location, it will open a second one at another site, and, if it has good name recognition, the second one may achieve quick customer acceptance. If it does not have name recognition, a long, hard struggle may be required to make it succeed. The question that must then be asked is, are the additional profits worth the additional burden of managing two locations?

Should You Franchise?

Many people think about franchising their business, but very few consider it seriously because it requires a great deal of legal and financial expertise, as well as a substantial amount of capital. One must be realistic in assessing whether the business is franchisable. Does it have universal appeal? Is it unique enough to fill an existing market niche?

Selling franchises is very different from selling food—is that what you want to do? Are you willing and able to take on the monumental volume of legal and marketing activities involved in franchising? Legal, accounting and marketing professionals should be consulted before any serious consideration is given to franchising.

Some restaurant companies prefer to open up additional company-owned locations as an alternative to franchising, with all of its complexities.

Should You Sell Your Restaurant?

If you are one of those people who enjoy the challenge of creating a successful restaurant but care very little about running it once the fun is over, you should consider selling it. There are individuals whose principal activity is starting, growing and selling restaurants for substantial gains on their investment.

If your restaurant is successful, you will be in the enviable position of being able to ask a higher price without having the financial pressure of needing to sell quickly.

You must ask yourself if you are happy with your lifestyle, and if you are getting the satisfaction you anticipated out of being in the restaurant business? If the answers to those questions are "no," you should probably sell the business and enjoy the profit from the sale. On the other hand, if the answers are "yes" and you remain in the business and continue to do a good job, you should make a very good living and be happy in your work.

Action Guidelines

✔ List your various options.

✔ Reassess your goals and objectives.

✔ Tabulate, in balance sheet form, the pros and cons of each option.

✔ Select the one that most closely matches your goals and objectives.

SAMPLE BUSINESS PLAN AND LOAN APPLICATION FOR A RESTAURANT

A well-organized and convincing business plan is essential for any business seeking to attract investors or to obtain funds from lenders. They will expect it to be complete, accurate and defendable.

A business plan should reflect conservative goals and expectations for the start-up period, and above all it must be believable. Following is an illustration of how a business plan for a medium-priced, full-service restaurant in an urban location might appear.

BUSINESS PLAN

THE BRANDING IRON STEAK HOUSE
50 Market Street
Capital City, MA 02202

January 10, 199–

Peter K. Public, Martha J. Public and Martin E. Public
120 State Street
Yourtown, MA 02206

Telephone:
(617) 000-0000

Copy No. 1

Table of Contents

PAGE

Statement of Purpose   **191**

Part One: The Business
- Background   191
- Mission Statement   192
- The Concept   192
- Location   192
- Industry Trends   193
- Other Resources   193
- The Management   193
- Objectives and Financial Expectations   194
- Product and Service   194
- Pricing and Profitability   194
- Product Life Cycle   195
- Market Analysis   195
- Competition   196
- Customers   196
- Marketing Strategy   197
- Personnel   197
- Risk   197
- Loan Request and Intended Use of Funds   200
- Summary of Part One   201

Part Two: Financial Projections
- Start-Up Requirements   201
- Estimated Annual Sales   202
- List of Furniture, Fixtures and Equipment   203
- Leasehold Improvements   204
- Sources and Uses of Funds   204
- Income Statement for First Year   205
- Projected Income Statement—Month by Month   206
- Cash Flow Statement—by Month   208

- Daily Breakeven Analysis   206
- Conclusion and Summary   207

Part Three: Supporting Documents   209
- Resumes of Partners   209
- Personal Balance Sheets of Partners   212
- Floor Plan of Resturant   214

STATEMENT OF PURPOSE

Peter K. Public, Martha J. Public and Martin E. Public, partners, seek a loan of $150,000, which together with their $150,000 personal investment, will be used to obtain a lease at 50 Market Street, Capital City, MA, acquire a liquor license, make improvements to the leased premises, purchase furniture, fixtures, equipment and inventories, provide working capital for two months and cover such other pre-opening expenses that are necessary to open The Branding Iron Steak House. It is expected that the business will produce a profit in the first year and increased profits are expected in subsequent years, assuring a timely payback of the loan.

PART ONE: THE BUSINESS

Background

The principals recognized a need for a full-service restaurant near the site of the new Megaplex Sports Center, which is scheduled to open in three months. The restaurant will be strategically located midway between several large parking garages, a subway station and the Megaplex entrance. It is estimated that since the new facility will house Capital City's four professional sports teams, there will be a year-round stream of several million fans walking directly by the restaurant each year.

Research disclosed there are only two restaurants and three bars within a two block radius of the Megaplex and one of them is a fast-food establishment and the other is a gourmet French restaurant. A survey of 1,500 sports fans revealed that a steak house would be most welcome at the new site.

The Branding Iron Steak House will occupy 3825 square feet of space at 50 Market Street and will have a capacity of 100 seats in its dining room and 36 seats in its lounge. Its hours of service will be 11 A.M. to midnight every day; however, dining room seating will cease at 10:30 P.M.

Entertainment will consist of two television sets located at the bar and electronic background music in the dining room. A piano player will play cocktail music in the lounge from 7 P.M. to 11 P.M., on Thursdays, Fridays and Saturdays.

Mission Statement

The Branding Iron Steak House seeks to serve high quality food and beverages in an upscale western atmosphere, conducive to family dining, while observing the highest standards of service.

The Concept

The Branding Iron Steak House will be a medium priced restaurant, featuring prompt service in a relaxing atmosphere. Its decor will be that of an early 1900s western beef house, with polished horse tack, pictures of cattle barons and famous cowboys decking the walls. The barnboard paneled walls and cedar-shingle roof façades will contrast with the luxurious carpeting and comfortable chairs in a way that will reflect the opulence of the cattle barons, as well as the rawhide lives of the cowboys. Lifesize pictures of famous bandits, "Wanted" signs, and front pages of old western newspapers will be displayed on the walls. Lighting will be provided by tiffany style light fixtures, and menu covers will be made of cowhide.

Location

The restaurant will be located at 50 Market Street in the east side of Capital City, an area that has been rehabilitated from a former produce market section into the site of Capital City's new Megaplex Sport Center. It will be housed in a small, renovated warehouse on the same street as the Megaplex Sports Center entrance, one-half block away. We can obtain a favorable seven-year lease with an option to renew. Occupancy costs will be $14.50 per square foot, on a triple net lease.

There are approximately 5,000 employees of neighboring businesses within a four-block area who are expected to patronize the restaurant from time to time.

In addition, the strategic location of the restaurant, midway between the Megaplex and the nearest parking garages and the subway station, assures that several million people will see the restaurant annually.

Access to The Branding Iron Steak House is available by taxi cab, subway, bus and automobile. The nearby parking garages provide parking for several thousand cars.

Industry Trends

Studies by three state and local governmental agencies indicate that the resurgence of economic growth in the greater Capital City area is expected to continue over the next decade, as a result of the entry of several high-tech industries into the area. The attractive pool of highly educated scientists, engineers and medical professionals in Capital City makes it an ideal location for such industries.

The expected industrial growth, coupled with the major boost the new Megaplex will give to the area's economy, will substantially benefit retail and hospitality businesses.

Other Resources

Lines of credit have been established with the following firms:

Central Meatpackers, Inc.	2/10, n/30
Standard Food Products, Co.	2/10, n/30
General Wares Equipment, Inc.	2/10, n/30

Professional services will be provided by the following firms:

Ryder & Hynes, Associates	Certified Public Accountants
Cooper, Kline & Calvin	Attorneys at Law
The Timkens Advertising Agency	Advertising
Restaurant Services, Inc.	Foodservice Consultants

The Management

The restaurant will be managed by Peter K. Public, who will also function as daytime bartender. Martin E. Public (Peter's brother) will be head chef and Martha J. Public (Peter's cousin) will be the dining room hostess.

Peter K. Public has eight years of experience as a bartender and head bartender for a prestigious Capital City restaurant, and six years of experience as the general manager of an upscale bar.

Martin E. Public has an associate degree in culinary arts. He has two years of experience as a first cook, four years as a sous chef and two years as night chef for a major hotel.

Martha J. Public has seven years of waitressing experience and five years of hostessing experience at an upscale restaurant in Chicago.

Objectives and Financial Expectations

The immediate goal of the management is to generate a cash flow sufficient to meet all obligations of the business and generate a net profit before taxes of 11 percent of total sales. It is expected this will be accomplished through creative merchandising, intensive advertising and the utilization of cost controls.

The long-term goal of the management is to become one of Capital City's culinary landmarks, yielding an annual return on investment in excess of 25 percent to its stockholders.

Product and Service

The Branding Iron Steak House will be unique to the Capital City area. Its style of service and method of food presentation will be similar to that of an upscale western beef house, and its unique western decor will be refreshingly appealing to the targeted clientele.

The clear message that The Branding Iron Steak House will strive to give is "this is a remarkable restaurant that serves excellent food and is convenient to the Megaplex." Its menu will feature a variety of steak, beef ribs, beef kabobs, chops and fried chicken for dinner, as well as a luncheon consisting of soups, steak sandwiches, gourmet burgers, salads plates and upscale appetizers. No other restaurant in the marketing area offers a similar menu.

Pricing and Profitability

The Branding Iron Steak House's dining room will operate with food cost percentage of 32 percent and its lounge will operate with a bar cost percentage of 23 percent.

The expected breakdown of total revenues will be 75 percent from food sales and 25 percent from beverage sales; the combined total cost of sales will be 29.7 percent. This produces a gross profit of 70.3 percent on total sales.

Prices will be competitive with comparable restaurants; however, the strategy of the Branding Iron Steak House will be to give a perception of higher value than its competitors, through its food and drink presentation methods.

Assuming a return on investment of at least 20.0 percent per year, the loan and the partner's investment will be recovered in five years or less.

Product Life Cycle

Due to the strategic location of the restaurant and the long-term loyalties of the sports fans that will go to the Megaplex Sports Center, The Branding Iron Steak House will have an indeterminate lifecycle, as long as its high standards of food and service are maintained.

At the end of the restaurant's fifth year, however, the management will conduct a self-study to ascertain whether the concept and the menu need to be rejuvenated.

It is anticipated that due to normal wear and tear, the facility will need a complete refurbishing and replacement of some equipment in seven years.

Market Analysis

The growth that will result from the opening of the new Megaplex Sports Center has been well determined by public and private researchers, and the restaurant will be in a strategic location to directly benefit from that growth.

The retail and office employees of nearby businesses and the increased number of retail shoppers and business people that will visit the area every business day are expected to try the restaurant.

Research indicates that after the Megaplex is opened, tour buses will bring thousands of sightseers into the area annually to see the unique architecture of the facility and to visit the many sports paraphernalia shops.

There are also seven colleges and universities, with a combined student body of over 100,000, located within a 30-minute subway ride.

Those who come to Megaplex events by subway will be delivered to the new station which is within view of the restaurant.

Surveys of both sports fans and employees of neighboring businesses revealed a desire for a nice place to eat near the Megaplex. The Branding Iron Steak House will fill this need and, at the present time, has no competition offering the same kind of food or concept within its marketing area.

Competition

There are two restaurants and three bars within a two-block radius of the Branding Iron Steak House and none of them is as accessible to the Megaplex.

One of the restaurants is a fast-food, hamburger-based establishment which caters mainly to youths and lower paid retail and service workers. The other is a high-priced, gourmet restaurant that features French cuisine.

Two of the bars are sports bar that serve only pizza and submarine sandwiches. The third one is a tavern that does not offer food.

Studies of the competitors showed that none of them presented substantial competition because of their different concepts and menu offerings.

Customers

The Branding Iron Steak House will have two types of customers.

1. Sports fans that will be going to the Megaplex
2. Retail and office employees, shoppers and tourists

Since the Megaplex will house hockey, basketball, baseball and football teams, it will generate a steady, year-round stream of potential customers.

The sports fans will typically be males and females over 18, from all walks of life, arriving as couples or in groups of two to four people, or family groups, with an average of two children, over eight years old.

The employees of nearby businesses will tend to commute by subway, while the shoppers will drive in from suburban communities and park in the garages.

Marketing Strategy

The Branding Iron Steak House will be positioned as a trendy place to have dinner on your way to or from a game at the Megaplex; a place where you can bring your business and social friends for an exceptionally good steak dinner and good drinks at attractive prices; a place where families will feel comfortable with their children.

In the evening, the bar will feature a piano player that will appeal to working people who seek a relaxing atmosphere, as well as to tourists and sports fans.

Public relations contacts will be made with taxicab companies, tour group leaders and other agencies that make recommendations to tourists.

All advertisements and commercials will position The Branding Iron Steak House as "the restaurant that must be tried when you visit Capital City." The Timkins Advertising Agency will handle all media placements and public relations releases. They have over 18 years of experience with top hospitality accounts in the Capital City area.

Support will be given to a few highly visible charitable organizations and community causes, and the partners of the business will be active members of the Chamber of Commerce, Rotary and Kiwanis clubs.

Personnel

The staff will include 11 full-time employees and 10 part-time employees, who will work an average of 638 hours per week, and generate a weekly payroll of $4,080.12 on average.

The estimated annual payroll of $212,166.24 is 26.4 percent of total sales. Table 1 shows the employee work schedule for The Branding Iron Steak House. Arrangements have been made for additional, temporary staffing on nights when special events are scheduled at the Megaplex.

Risk

Risk management will be practiced from the opening day. All food service handlers will be given an in-house food sanitation and safety course and all servers will be required to attend an accredited

EMPLOYEE WORK SCHEDULE

	Mon.	Tue.	Wed.	Thur.	Fri.	Sat.	Sun.	Total Hours	Hourly Rate	Weekly Pay
BAR PERSONNEL										
Day Head Bartender	10/6	10/6	10/6	10/6	10/6			40	9.82	392.80
Night Head Bartender	11/2		5/1	5/1	5/1	5/1	5/1	40	7.00	280.00
Bartender, Part time		11/2	11/2	11/2	11/2			15	6.00	90.00
Bartender, Part time			6/9	6/9	6/1	6/1	6/10	24	5.50	132.00
Bartender, Part time	5/1	5/1				10/6	10/6	32	5.50	176.00
Bartender, Part time	6/9	6/9				11/2	11/2	12	5.50	66.00
WAIT STAFF										
Day Head Waitperson	10/4		10/4	10/4	10/4	10/4	10/4	36	5.42	195.12
Night Head Waitperson		4/10	4/10	4/10	4/10	4/10	4/10	36	3.25	117.00
Waitperson, Part time	11/2	10/4	11/2	11/2	11/2			18	2.95	53.10
Waitperson, Part time	4/10	11/2	11/2	11/2	11/2			18	2.95	53.10
Waitperson, Part time	11/2				11/2	11/2		12	2.95	35.40
Waitperson, Part time		5/9	5/9	5/10	5/10	11/2	11/2	24	2.95	70.80

	Day 1	Day 2	Day 3	Day 4	Day 5	Day 6	Day 7	Hours	Rate	Weekly Total
Waitperson, Part time	5/9		5/9	5/9	5/9	5/10	5/9	21	2.95	61.95
Waitperson, Part time						5/10	5/9	13	2.95	38.35
KITCHEN PERSONNEL										
Head Chef		9/5	9/5	9/5	9/5	9/5	9/5	48	12.00	576.00
Night Chef	5/12	5/12	5/12	5/12	5/12	5/12	5/12	40	9.31	372.30
Rounds Person	9/5	5/10	5/10	11/7	11/7	11/7	5/11	40	8.00	320.00
Cooks Helper	4/11	4/11		4/11	4/11	4/11	4/11	48	6.75	324.00
Salad Maker	11/7	11/7	11/7		11/7	11/7	11/7	48	6.75	324.00
Dishwasher & Porter	11/4	11/4	11/4	11/5			11/5	32	6.00	192.00
Dishwasher	5/10	5/10	5/10	5/10	5/10	5/10		30	7.00	210.00

Total Weekly Payroll $ 4,080.12
Times 52 weeks x 52
EST. ANNUAL PAYROLL $212,166.24

Table 1: Estimated Annual Payroll of The Branding Iron Steak House

Responsible Alcohol Service Course. Both courses will entitle the restaurant to substantial discounts on insurance premiums. The Branding Iron Steak House will carry the following insurances:

Named Peril Insurance
Liquor Liability and Third Party Liability Insurance
Workers Compensation Insurance
General Liability Insurance
Business Interruption Insurance
Product Liability Insurance
Fire insurance
Key Person Life Insurance on partners
Personal Injury Liability Insurance

In addition to insuring against specific risks, ongoing training programs will be conducted to assure high degree of professionalism among employees in their respective jobs.

Loan Request and Intended Use of Funds

Amount Requested: $150,000

Term of Loan: 15 years; first payment due three months after transaction date of loan.

Interest Rate: 12% fixed rate, with no prepayment penalty.

Debt to Equity Ratio: 1 to 1 ($150,000 to $150,000)

Collateral: Deed of trust on the wholly owned home of Peter K. Public. Current market value appraised at $225,000.

Other Protections: Borrowers will carry insurance against business interruption and loss due to hazards, naming the lender as a beneficiary in the event of interruption of business.

Intended Use of Funds: The partners will use the borrowed funds, in conjunction with their own investment, to acquire a license, secure a lease, make improvements to the leased premises, purchase the furniture, fixtures, equipment and inventories necessary to open The Branding Iron Steak House and to conduct a grand opening.

Summary of Part One

Peter K. Public, along with his brother, Martin E. Public, and his cousin, Martha J. Public (equal partners), seek a secured loan of $150,000 which, in conjunction with their combined personal investment of $150,000, will be used to open an upscale western style steak house, to be known as The Branding Iron Steak House, at 50 Market Street, Capital City, MA.

Extensive market analysis indicates there is a need for such a restaurant and a sufficient target population to sustain it. The new Megaplex Sports Center, which will be located a half block away, is expected to bring a minimum of 2,000,000 people into the area every year.

The restaurant will have a capacity of 100 seats in its dining room and 36 seats in its lounge. It will offer high-quality food and beverage service in a unique, casual but comfortable, atmosphere. Its rustic decor will resemble an early 1900s, upscale, western beef house. There is no direct competition in its dominant marketing area.

It is expected that through effective sales promotion, rigid training and the use of cost controls, the restaurant will be profitable from the first year and will be able to pay back the loan and the partner's investment in five years.

PART TWO: FINANCIAL PROJECTIONS

Start-Up Requirements

Cash (Working Capital)	$16,000
Leasehold Improvements	75,100
License	32,000
Beginning Inventories	20,900
(Food, Beverages and Supplies)	
Furniture, Fixtures and Equipment	130,500
Opening Expenses	25,500
(Liquor liability insurance, other insurances,	

licenses, permits, clean up, advertising and
promotion, deposits, employee training, preopening
parties and grand opening)

Total Start-Up Investment Required   **$300,000**

Estimated Annual Sales

Number of Customers Expected Each Day of the Week

	Mon.	Tue.	Wed.	Thur.	Fri.	Sat.	Sun.	Total
Lunch	75	75	80	90	100	90	80	590
Dinner	35	45	60	65	85	90	75	455
Bar Only	20	25	40	50	65	70	25	295

Total Customers per Week   1340

Average Menu Prices

Sandwiches and Salads	$ 4.75
Entrees	10.95
Desserts	2.50
Drinks	2.75

Estimated Average Guest Check Per Person

Lunch	Sandwich or Salad plus .5 Drinks*	$ 6.13
Dinner	Entree, Salad, .5 Dessert, plus 2 Drinks	22.45
Bar Only	Average 2 Drinks	5.50

Estimated Weekly Sales

590 lunch customers	×	$ 6.13	=	3,617
455 dinner customers	×	22.45	=	10,215
295 bar only customers	×	5.50	=	1,623

Total Weekly Sales   **$15,455**

Estimated Annual Sales

52 weeks   × $15,455   = $803,660

*Note: The .5 for items such as dessert and drinks allows for the expectation that only one out of every two customers will order one of those items.

List of Furniture, Fixtures and Equipment

Qty.	Item	Cost
1	Walk-in Refrigerator	$ 7,100
1	Dishwasher, automatic	11,300
1	Freezer, reach in, stainless, with racks	3,725
2	Fryers, twin basket	7,450
1	Griddle, 3'	3,500
1	Toaster, automatic, conveyor type	1,725
2	Stainless steel prep tables	800
1	Food Mixer, 20 quart	3,175
2	Restaurant ranges	4,850
1	Convection Oven	5,450
1	Garbage Disposer	300
2	Refrigerators, 40 cu. ft., stainless	4,475
1	Fire protection hood and exhaust system	10,000
1	Broiler	2,800
1	Coffee Urn	2,100
1	Ice Maker, air cooled, 600-pound capacity	3,000
1	Remote, 6-keg capacity, beer refrigerator	2,500
2	Cocktail stations, 30"	1,800
2	Three compartment bar sinks, with speed racks and double drain boards	1,500
1	Direct draw, 3-keg beer box, with taps	2,100
2	Post mix soda dispensing systems, with carbonator and 50' lines	2,000
1	Three door bar refrigerator	2,400
1	Glass froster, 3', 120-mug capacity	1,200
1	Beer bottle cooler, 4'	900
20'	Front Bar with top and foot rail	4,020
14'	Back Bar with cabinets and shelves	2,038
15	Bar Stools, upholstered	3,901
8	Booths, 4'	4,013
12	Tables, with bases, seat 4	2,388
10	Tables, with bases, seat 2	1,750
100	Chairs	12,500
2	Television sets	4,500
	Glassware	1,100
	Small wares and supplies	1,800

1	Safe, fireproof	2,500
1	Cash register	2,250
1	Desk, mahogany and swivel chair	625
1	Desk, steel and secretary's chair	450
1	Planter, divider, 3' high	515

Total Cost of Furniture, Fixtures and Equipment   **$130,500**

Leasehold Improvements

Heating, Ventilation and Air Conditioning	$20,280
Electrical	17,920
Plumbing	14,100
Carpeting, Floor Tile and other related equipment	22,800

Total Leasehold Improvements   **$75,100**

Sources and Uses of Funds

USES OF FUNDS	SOURCE OF FUNDS		
Start up Expenses	**Partners' Equity**	**Loan**	**Total**
Furniture, Fixtures and Equipment	$65,250	$65,250	$130,500
Leasehold Improvements	37,550	37,550	75,100
License	32,000	0	32,000
Food, Beverage and Supplies Inventories	10,450	10,450	20,900
Opening Expenses	12,750	12,750	25,500
(Liquor liability insurance, other insurances, licenses, permits, advertising, lease deposit, clean up, employee training, preopening parties and grand opening)			
Working Capital	8,000	8,000	16,000
Total Funds	**$166,000**	**$134,000**	**$300,000**

Income Statement for First Year (January 1 through December 31, 199—)

		Pct.
Sales		
Food Sales	$602,745	75.0%
Beverage Sales	200,915	25.0
Total Sales	**$803,660**	**100.0**
Cost of Sales		
Food Cost	$192,878	32.0
Beverage Cost	46,210	23.0
Total Cost of Sales	**$239,088**	**29.7**
Gross Profit from Operations	**$564,572**	**70.3**
Other Income	2,411	0.3
Total Income	**$566,983**	**70.6**
Controllable Expenses		
Payroll	$212,166	26.4
Employee Benefits	32,146	4.0
Direct Operating Expenses	45,809	5.7
Advertising and Promotion	23,306	2.9
Music and Entertainment	16,073	2.0
Utilities	25,717	3.2
Administrative and General Expenses	32,146	4.0
Repairs and Maintenance	16,073	2.0
Total Controllable Expenses	**$403,436**	**50.2**
Profit Before Occupancy Costs	**$163,547**	**20.4**
Occupancy Costs (Triple Net Lease)		
Rent	$ 40,987	5.1
Property Taxes	4,822	0.6
Other Taxes	1,607	0.2
Property Insurance	8,037	1.0
Total Occupancy Costs	**$ 55,453**	**6.9**
Profit Before Interest and Depreciation	**$108,094**	**13.5**
Interest	4,018	0.5
Depreciation	16,075	2.0
Net Profit	**$ 88,001**	**11.0**

Projected Income Statement—Month by Month

	JAN	FEB	MAR	APR	MAY
Sales					
Food	45,653	46,556	47,229	48,730	47,978
Beverage	15,218	15,519	15,743	16,243	15,993
Total Sales	60,870	62,074	62,972	64,973	63,971
Cost of Sales					
Food	14,609	14,898	15,113	15,594	15,353
Beverage	3,500	3,569	3,621	3,736	3,678
Total Cost of Sales	18,109	18,467	18,734	19,330	19,031
Gross Profit from Operations	42,761	43,607	44,238	45,644	44,940
Other Income	183	186	189	195	192
Total Income	42,944	43,793	44,427	45,839	45,132
Controllable Expenses					
Payroll	16,070	16,388	16,625	17,153	16,888
Employee Benefits	2,435	2,483	2,519	2,599	2,559
Direct Operating	3,470	3,538	3,589	3,703	3,646
Advertising and Promotion	1,765	1,800	1,826	1,884	1,855
Music and Entertainment	1,217	1,241	1,259	1,299	1,279
Utilities	1,948	1,986	2,015	2,079	2,047
Administrative and Gen.	2,435	2,483	2,519	2,599	2,559
Repairs and Maintenance	1,217	1,241	1,259	1,299	1,279
Total Controllable Expenses	30,557	31,161	31,612	32,616	32,113
Profit Before Occupancy Costs	12,387	12,632	12,815	13,222	13,018
Occupancy Costs					
Rent	3,416	3,416	3,416	3,416	3,416
Property Taxes	365	372	378	390	384
Other Taxes	122	124	126	130	128
Property Insurance	609	621	630	650	640
Total Occupancy Costs	4,511	4,533	4,549	4,585	4,567
Profit Before Int. and Depr.	7,876	8,099	8,266	8,637	8,451
Interest	304	310	315	325	320
Depreciation	1,217	1,241	1,259	1,299	1,279
NET PROFIT BEFORE TAXES	6,354	6,547	6,691	7,013	6,852

Daily Breakeven Analysis

Monthly Fixed Costs

Rent	$ 3,416
Salaries	9,548
Utilities	2,143
Insurance	1,055
Taxes	2,086
Depreciation	1,339
Total Monthly Fixed Costs	**$19,587**

Daily Fixed Costs (Total Monthly Fixed Cost ÷ 30 days) $ 653

Daily Variable Costs

Cost of Food (one day's supply)	$ 528
Cost of Liquor (one day's supply)	127
Cost of Additional Staff Essential to Sales	355
Total Daily Variable Costs	**$1,010**

Daily Sales Volume Required To Break Even   **$ 1,663**

The Branding Iron Steak House
Projected Income Statement
by Month for One Year
January 1 - December 31, 199—

JUN	JUL	AUG	SEP	OCT	NOV	DEC	TOTAL
49,480	50,978	51,736	52,475	53,149	54,055	54,728	602,745
16,493	16,993	17,246	17,491	17,716	18,018	18,243	200,915
65,973	67,971	68,982	69,966	70,865	72,073	72,970	803,660
15,834	16,313	16,556	16,792	17,008	17,298	17,513	192,878
3,793	3,908	3,966	4,023	4,075	4,144	4,196	46,210
19,627	20,221	20,522	20,815	21,082	21,442	21,709	239,089
46,346	47,750	48,460	49,151	49,783	50,631	51,261	564,571
198	204	207	210	213	216	219	2,411
46,544	47,954	48,667	49,361	49,995	50,848	51,480	566,982
17,417	17,944	18,211	18,471	18,708	19,027	19,264	212,166
2,639	2,719	2,759	2,799	2,835	2,883	2,919	32,146
3,760	3,874	3,932	3,988	4,039	4,108	4,159	45,809
1,913	1,971	2,000	2,029	2,055	2,090	2,116	23,306
1,319	1,359	1,380	1,399	1,417	1,441	1,459	16,073
2,111	2,175	2,207	2,239	2,268	2,306	2,335	25,717
2,639	2,719	2,759	2,799	2,835	2,883	2,919	32,146
1,319	1,359	1,380	1,399	1,417	1,441	1,459	16,073
33,118	34,121	34,629	35,123	35,574	36,181	36,631	403,437
13,426	13,832	14,038	14,238	14,421	14,667	14,849	163,545
3,416	3,416	3,416	3,416	3,416	3,416	3,416	40,987
396	408	414	420	425	432	438	4,822
132	136	138	140	142	144	146	1,607
660	680	690	700	709	721	730	8,037
4,603	4,639	4,657	4,675	4,691	4,713	4,729	55,453
8,822	9,193	9,381	9,563	9,730	9,954	10,120	108,092
330	340	345	350	354	360	365	4,018
1,319	1,359	1,380	1,399	1,417	1,441	1,459	16,073
7,173	7,494	7,656	7,814	7,958	8,152	8,296	88,001

Conclusion and Summary

This request is for a secured loan in the amount of $150,000, which together with an investment of $150,000 by Peter K. Public, Martha J. Public and Martin E. Public (equal partners), will be used to start The Branding Iron Steak House. Specifically, the funds will be used to acquire a license, obtain a lease for premises at 50 Market Street, purchase furniture, fixtures, equipment and inventories, hire and train a staff, for preopening expenses and as working capital.

All financial projections have been made conservatively, with a 10 percent safety factor used to overstate costs and to understate revenues. It is expected that The Branding Iron Steak House will operate profitably in its first year of operation and be able to meet all of its obligations in a timely manner.

CASH FLOW STATEMENT – BY MONTH (Jan. 1- Dec. 31, 199-)

SOURCES OF CASH	PREOPENING	JAN	FEB	MAR	APR	MAY	JUN	JUL	AUG	SEPT	OCT	NOV	DEC	TOTAL
Partner's Equity	150,000													150,000
Loan	150,000													150,000
Net Profit	0	4,855	4,965	5,045	5,135	5,275	5,395	6,512	7,450	9,505	10,425	11,485	12,216	88,263
Depreciation	0	1,450	1,450	1,450	1,450	1,450	1,450	1,450	1,450	1,450	1,450	1,450	1,450	17,400
TOTAL	300,000	6,305	6,415	6,495	6,585	6,725	6,845	7,962	8,900	10,955	11,875	12,935	13,666	405,663
DISBURSEMENTS														
Liquor License	32,000													32,000
Leasehold Improv.	75,100													75,100
Furn./Fix./Equip.	130,500													130,500
Beg. Inventories	20,900													20,900
Opening Costs	25,500													25,500
Mo. Loan Paymts.	0	0	1,833	1,833	1,833	1,833	1,833	1,833	1,833	1,833	1,833	1,833	1,833	20,163
Income Taxes	0	1,074	1,476	1,580	2,182	2,284	2,387	2,492	3,098	3,400	4,105	3,109	4,076	31,263
TOTAL	284,000	1,074	3,309	3,413	4,015	4,117	4,220	4,325	4,931	5,233	5,938	4,942	5,909	335,426
MO. CASH FLOW	16,000	5,231	3,106	3,082	2,570	2,608	2,625	3,637	3,969	5,722	5,937	7,993	7,757	70,237
CUM. CASH FLOW	16,000	21,231	24,337	27,419	29,989	32,597	35,222	38,859	42,828	48,550	54,487	62,480	70,237	70,237

The opening of the nearby Megaplex Sports Center will attract several million sports fans and tourists to the dominant marketing area of The Branding Iron Steak House each year. In addition, a program of aggressive marketing and strict cost controls should enable the restaurant's profits to grow for the foreseeable future.

Based on the foregoing documentation and the research upon which it is based, the proposed restaurant should be viable and able to meet all of its obligations in a timely manner, as well as to generate a very satisfactory return for its owners.

PART THREE: SUPPORTING DOCUMENTS

Resumes of Partners

Peter K. Public
120 State Street
Yourtown, MA 02206
Tel. (617) 000-0000

Education:
Western Regional High School, Center Field, MA

Employment:
The Puritan Restaurant, Capital City, MA, 1980-1988
Position, Bartender and Head Bartender

Mystic River Lounge, 1988-1995
Position: General Manager

Personal Credit References:
Onshore Savings Bank
House mortgage, paid up in 1992

Second Federal Bank, Capital City, MA
Automobile Loan, 24 months, paid up, 1994

Personal: Born: May 20, 1954, Camtree, MA
Married, wife's name Elizabeth, one son, Avery

References:

Thomas Bacon, President	Barry Lender, Sales Manager
First Institute of Savings	Viable Insurance Co.
1503 Flint Street	520 Granite Road
Capital City, MA 02200	Capital City, MA 02200

Martha J. Public
23 Byfield Street
Yourtown, MA 02209
Tel. (617) 000-0000

Education:
Broader College, Chicago, IL
Liberal Arts, 1985

Employment:
The Top of the Loop Restaurant, Chicago, IL 1983-1995
Positions: Waitress, Head Waitress, Hostess

Personal Credit References:
Windy City Savings Bank, Chicago, IL
Automobile loan, paid up in 1995

Uptown Finance Co., Capital City, MA
Personal Loan, 12 months, paid up, 1994

References:
Alice Maxfield, Executive Director
Bayside Charities Inc.
390 Pondview Street
Moreland, MA 02207

Charles Bookman, Manager
Flashwell Accounting Services
17 Jackson Street
Chicago, IL 02203

Martin E. Public
1123 Central Street
Yourtown, MA 02209
Tel. (617) 000-0000

Education:
Harbor Community College, Capital City, MA
A.S. Culinary Arts, 1985

Employment:
Pilgrim Hotel, Capital City, MA, 1986-1995
Positions: First Cook, Sous Chef, Night Chef

Personal Credit References:
Bayside Savings Bank
Automobile loan, paid up in 1993

Uptown National Bank, Capital City, MA
Boat Loan, 36 months, paid up, 1992

References:
Ann Carswell, Executive Director
Bayside Chamber of Commerce
690 Water Street
Capital City, MA 02202

Calvin Binder, Advertising Manager
Finer & Hapwell Advertising Agency
417 Maryland Street
Capital City, MA 02203

Personal Balance Sheets of Partners

Peter K. Public
(as of November 1, 199–)

ASSETS

Cash in Bank—Savings	$ 8,000
Checking	3,000
Marketable Securities	75,000
Life Insurance	35,000
Real Estate (Current Market Value)	225,000
Automobile	22,500
Other personal assets	21,000
TOTAL ASSETS	**$389,500**

LIABILITIES

Accounts Payable	$ 3,400
Automobile Installment Loan	18,000
Home Improvement Loan	39,000
TOTAL LIABILITIES	**$60,400**
NET WORTH	**$329,100**
TOTAL LIABILITIES AND NET WORTH	**$389,500**

Martin E. Public
(as of November 1, 199–)

ASSETS

Cash in Bank—Savings	$12,200
Checking	2,000
Marketable Securities	40,000
Automobile	12,000
Other personal assets	8,000
TOTAL ASSETS	**$74,200**

LIABILITIES

Accounts Payable	$ 3,500
Automobile Installment Loan	8,400
TOTAL LIABILITIES	**$11,900**
NET WORTH	**$62,300**
TOTAL LIABILITIES AND NET WORTH	**$74,200**

Martha J. Public
(as of November 1, 199–)

ASSETS

Cash in Bank—Savings	$ 28,200
Checking	7,000
Marketable Securities	90,000
Automobile	17,000
Other personal assets	18,000
TOTAL ASSETS	**$160,200**

LIABILITIES

Accounts Payable	$ 3,500
Automobile Installment Loan	12,400
TOTAL LIABILITIES	**$15,900**
NET WORTH	**$144,300**
TOTAL LIABILITIES AND NET WORTH	**$160,200**

Floor Plan of Restaurant

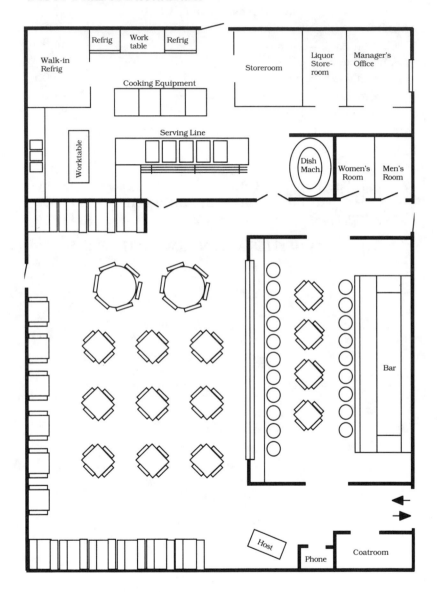

Index

A

Abbreviations, 82
Acid test ratio, 140
Advertising, analysis, 162–165;
   media, 161
Aisles, 76, 95
Alcohol, responsibility, 177
Automated systems, 144
Average guest check, 141

B

Back of house, 86
Balance sheet, 136
Bar, design, 84
Bureau of Alcohol, Tobacco
   and Firearms, BATF, 22
Buddy system, 81
Business entity, 37
Business plan, 46;
   how to construct, 50–55;
   outline of, 48–49;
   sample, 187–214

C

Capital, acquiring, 40

Certificate of Occupancy, 20
Cherry picking, 102
Chinaware, 95
Cleaning, sanitizing, 174
Closing the deal, 37
Communications, 129
Competitive buying, 101
Concentration strategy, 154
Cooperation, employee, 127
Corporation, 39
Current ratio, 139
Customer service, 83

D

Demographics, 149–150, 152
Differentiation strategy, 153

E

Entertainment, breakeven point,
   117;
   types of, 115
Equipment; bar, 85; dining room, 78;
   kitchen, 90, 94; maintenance,
   117; selection factors, 88
Expansion, 184

Expense percentages, 139
Environment, decor, 72

F

Federal requirements, 22
Financing, sources of, 14
Fire, safety, 176
Floor plan, guidelines for, 78; layout,
    76
Food cost percentage, 138
Franchise, 185

G

General partner, 38
Geographic information, 149–150,
    152
Glassware, 95
Grand opening, 155–157

H

Hidden agendas, 129

I

Identification cards, 181
Image, 160
Income statement, 133–135
Insurance, types of, 44
Interviews, employee, 124
Intoxication, signs of, 177
Inventory, categories of, 100;
    sheet, 104; turnover rate, 99
Issuing, 105

J

Job description, 130–131

L

Labor cost percentage, 138
Labor turnover, 121
Lease, equipment, 93
Licenses, food service 16;
    liquor, 21
Life cycle, business, 148–149

Limited partner, 38
Liquor laws, 180
Location, selection of, 40

M

Maintenance, equipment, 118
Manager, role of, 9–10
Market penetration, 153
Marketing plan, 146–147
Market quotation sheet, 102
Market research, 149
Menus, children's, 60; developing,
    57; format, 58–60; limitations,
    58; methods of pricing, 61–64;
    truth in, 60; types of, 56–57
Morale, employee, 128

N

Name, selection of, 43
National Sanitation Foundation, 175
Net profit on sales, 139

O

Organization, operational, 74–75
Orientation, employee, 124–126

P

Par stock, 109
Partnerships, 38
Payroll, analysis, 122–123
Permits, fire, 18–19; building, 19–20
Pest control, 175
Popularity index, 112
Pouring cost percentage, 138
Production planning, 111
Production system, 89
Professional assistance, 37
Profit centers, 97
Pricing, beer, 68; food, 61–64;
    mixed drinks, 69–70; wines, 67
Psychographic information,
    149–150, 152
Publicity, free, 157–158

Purchase order, 103
Purchasing, 98, 172

R

Ratios, analytical, 137
Receiving, 105, 173
Receiving clerk's report, 106
Requirements, financial 13–14;
location, 15–16; legal, 16;
personal, 15
Requisition, 109
Rent, factors, 33
Responsible business practices, 179
Restaurant, evaluation, 35; history,
1–3; ownership, 11–12; types
of, 8–9
Return on investment, 139
Risk management, 43–44

S

Safety, employee, 175; customer, 176
Sales, establishing goals, 165–167;
history, 110–111
Sanitation, food, 172
Seat turnover ratio, 141
Selling, business, 185
Service bar, 85
Service system, 79–80
Sidework, 81
Simple control system, 142
Skimming market, 63
Sole proprietorship, 38

Space allocation, dining room, 75–76;
kitchen, 87
Special events, themes, 159–160
Special Occupational Tax Stamp, 23
Specials, menu, 64
Standards, 61, 98
Standardized recipes, 110
Start-up, activities, 30; costs, 47
State approval agencies, 20
Stock record card, 108
Storing, 105; food, 173
Strategies, competitive, 153–154
Supervision, employee, 112

T

Tables, selection factors, 79
Target market, 151–152
Telephone selling, 170
Training, employee, 126–127

U

Under capitalization, 25
Undesirable practices, 143

V

Valuation, methods of, 32
Vendors, working with, 87

W

Wine list, design, 65
Work center, layout, 90–91, 92
Working capital, 140